Marketing for Tourism

Related Macmillan titles

The New Catering Repertoire   H. L. Cracknell and G. Nobis
 Volume 1   Aide-Mémoire du Chef
 Volume 2   Aide-Mémoire du Restaurateur et Sommelier
Practical Professional Catering   H. L. Cracknell, G. Nobis and
                                                              R. Kaufmann
Practical Professional Cookery   H. L. Cracknell and R. Kaufmann
Practical Professional Gastronomy   H. L. Cracknell and G. Nobis
Managing Food Hygiene   Nicholas Johns
Healthy Eating: a guide for chefs and caterers   Rob Silverstone

**In the Mastercraft series, published with the Hotel and Catering
Training Company:**

Customercraft: Keeping the Customer Satisfied   Roy Apps
Foodcraft 1: The Dry Processes
Foodcraft 2: The Wet Processes
*Mastercraft 1: Working in the Hotel and
                           Catering Industry*   Sally Messenger
*Mastercraft 2: Health, Hygiene and Safety
                           in the Hotel and Catering Industry*   Marion Kenber and
                                                                                 William McCurrach

Professional Masters – all the professional student needs – in a single text:

Basic English Law   W. T. Major
Communication   Nicki Stanton
Company Accounting   Roger Oldcorn
Cost and Management Accounting   Roger Hussey
Employee Relations   Chris Brewster
Management   Roger Oldcorn
Marketing   Robert I. Maxwell
Personal Management   Margaret Attwood
Study Skills   Kate Williams
Supervision   Mike Savedra and John Hawthorn

Please write to the Sales Department, Macmillan Education, Houndmills,
Basingstoke, Hants, for details of other Mastercraft titles, other Macmillan
textbooks and the current Further and Continuing Education catalogue.

Marketing for Tourism
Case Study Assignments

Les Lumsdon

Foreword by Wyn Mears

MACMILLAN

First published 1992 by
MACMILLAN EDUCATION LTD
Houndmills, Basingstoke, Hampshire RG21 2XS
and London
Companies and representatives
throughout the world

ISBN 0–333–54136–7

A catalogue record for this book is available
from the British Library.

Copy-edited and typeset by Povey/Edmondson
Okehampton and Rochdale, England

Printed in Hong Kong

Contents

Foreword

The marketing of tourism has now reached its maturity in the sense that it is recognised, not only as an accepted and very necessary business practice in its own right, but also because of the way in which it has developed its own distinct academic disciplines. Whilst it is often accepted that the principle of 'marketing' as a philosophy can be equally well applied to any business situation, and that 'marketeers' should be equally adept at applying their skills to any product, there is increasing evidence that even within the field of marketing, specialists are emerging in their own particular spheres, and that careers are being forged in distinct sectors of industry.

Travel and tourism are areas in which specialist market training is becoming essential for graduate entrants, and the emergence of specialised marketing-orientated courses and modules at colleges and universities throughout the world is evidence both of the wide range of opportunities that is now available to young people looking to enter the industry, and of the industry's own need to employ staff with sound, well-informed backgrounds.

Further evidence of the industry's maturity may now be found along the bookshelves of classified 'tourism' sections of college libraries and academic bookshops. Several excellent 'tourism marketing' text books and studies have been published in recent years providing indispensable foundations for teachers and students alike and closing important gaps that had been crying out to be filled for some time. The publication of *Marketing for Tourism* has come at an opportune time to complement this range as it provides the essential bridge between the theory of tourism marketing and the real day-to-day situations where training and academic though processes are put into practice. Practitioners as well as college students will find the diverse examples illustrated in this book to be of real value in demonstrating that there is rarely a 'model' situation in tourism marketing: situations are not often repeatable in an identical way, and there cannot often be standard marketing plans and campaigns which provide identical solutions to similar problems. This is, of course, one of the great joys of marketing which provides marketeers with guaranteed excitement and day-to-day challenges – they never disappoint and always provide high degrees of motivation!

Nevertheless, the approaches adopted by each of the case studies will stimulate readers to learn from the experience of operators in the public and private sectors of travel and tourism and enable them to adopt at least some of these experiences in their own future marketing planning requirements.

WYN MEARS
(formerly UK Marketing Director, Wales Tourist Board, now with BBC Wales)

Acknowledgements

The author wishes to thank the organisations and companies concerned for their assistance in the preparation of the cases, and to colleagues at Staffordshire Polytechnic including Simon Seward (past M.Sc. Research student), Jonathan Swift, John Wetwood and Ian Wilson who gave advice on the case study material. My sincere gratitude is also extended to dozens of past students who have taught me so much about case studies.

The author wishes to thank Wyn Mears, formerly UK Marketing Director, Wales Tourist Board and now with BBC Wales, for writing the foreword to this volume.

The cover illustration reproduces Eilean Donan Castle's *The Highlands*, © British Tourist Authority/English Tourist Board/Syndication International.

The author also wishes to thank numerous colleagues within the following organisations and companies for assisting in the preparation of the twelve case studies and for granting permission to use appropriate material in each instance:

Air Miles
British Tourist Authority
Co-op Travelcare
Granada Studios Tours
Great British City Breaks
L&R Leisure plc and Merseytravel
Peak District National Park
Torbay Tourist Board
Transport for Leisure
Trusthouse Forte[*]
Wales Tourist Board
Youth Hostels Association (England and Wales)

[*]Since the case-study was prepared, THF have changed their corporate identity to Forte.

Introduction: Marketing for Tourism

Tourism Marketing

Is there a 'Tourist industry'? Many writers suggest not. Jefferson and Lickorish,[1] for example, refer to it as a market and not a single industry. Mill and Morrison[2] describe it as a phenomenon, Burkart and Medlik[3] a composite phenomenon. Holloway and Plant[4] use a range of terms in their introductory chapter, referring to the 'tourism business', the 'tourism industry' and 'tourism services', as do many authors when introducing the nature of the Tourism business.

It is difficult to describe tourism, or 'travel and tourism' as Middleton[5] refers to it, as an industry because this suggests that it is more unified than it really is. It is not like the coal or the brewing industry. There is not the clearly defined structure found elsewhere.

The business of tourism may be described as a collection of service activities. There is a certain degree of cohesion in that organisations such as Tourist Boards and other interested bodies attempt to co-ordinate different business activities embracing tourism, but the fragmentation remains. There are several reasons for this.

For many businesses in tourism, looking after the visitor is not the primary activity. A transport undertaking, for example, might be interested mainly in serving the needs of the commuter but have a secondary remit to meet the needs of visitors. A local inn might look to its regular residents for 90 per cent of its trade, serving the needs of visitors as a marginal activity only. Given that many of the businesses involved in tourism are multi-faceted and multi-market-based it is difficult to envisage a cohesive industry. Another key reason is that governments have tended not to see tourism as a decisive commercial force, and hence their interest in tourism-related activities has been the province of several departments – Trade and Industry, Employment and Environment – and has offered less than clear policy statements about the role of tourism within the overall economic structure.

Business Sector

When it comes to classification, tourism is best referred to as a business sector, reflecting the fact that it is many 'businesses' with differing activities wholly or partly involved in servicing the needs of visitors. The scale and scope of this sector is outlined in Tables A, B and C. Most commentators now agree that it is of considerable importance in a social and economic sense.

Table A   Tourism in England by British residents

	Trips	Nights	Spending (£m)
1983	110	435	£4,300
1984	113	440	£4,525
1984*	116	450	£4,800
1985	105	400	£5,075
1986	106	405	£5,600
1987	110	400	£5,550
1988	110	410	£6,275

* In this year the data were calculated in a different manner.

Source: English Tourist Board, *Insights*, Table 1 (1990).

Table B   Overseas visitors to the UK (trips in 000)

		Area of visit		
year	Total (000s)	North America	Western Europe	Other areas
1987	15,566	3,394	9,317	2,855
1988 R	15,798	3,272	9,668	2,859
% Change 1987/1988	+1	−4	+4	−

Source: English Tourist Board, *Insights*, Table 1 (1990).

Table C   Visits abroad by UK residents (trips in 000s)

		Area of visit		
year	Total (000s)	North America	Western Europe	Other areas
1987	27,447	1,559	23.678	2,210
1988R	28,828	1,823	24,519	2,486
% Change 1987/1988	+5	+17	+4	+11

Source: English Tourist Board, *Insights*, Table 2 (1990).

Definition

A useful general definition is provided by the Tourism Society:[6]

> Tourism is deemed to include any activity concerned with the temporary short-term movement of people to destinations outside the places where they normally live and work, and their activities during the stay at these destinations.

As Middleton[7] points out, this definition is not peculiarly British, it is global in its appeal and strength. It is about how pleasure, VFR (Visiting Friends and Relatives) or business trips are encouraged (or, in some instances, discouraged), managed, serviced and monitored. Marketing has an important role to play in this business sector, and it is essential to understand the marketing management process. Martin[8] describes the broad process which any firm or organisation in tourism will go through.

1. They will analyse their current situation to see where they are going.
2. They will state where they would like to be by defining their objectives and assessing the discrepancy/gap between these two.

3. Some broad strategies will be devised to help ensure that the firm will end up where it wishes to be rather than where it is headed at the moment. The bigger the gap which emerges from steps 1 and 2 the more dramatic/risky are the strategies likely to be.
4. Finally some detailed planning will be necessary to implement these strategies and a control mechanism devised to monitor these plans.

Marketing Planning

Market planning is crucial to the survival of any business in the long run, and several of the case studies in this text draw the reader's attention to the importance of developing marketing strategies and action plans to meet objectives. In particular, Case 1, The Wales Tourist Board, brings key marketing planning issues into focus.

The tourism marketeer spends too little time in this sphere, mainly because he or she is too busy making things happen on the ground, preparing for exhibitions, agreeing the fine details of a sales promotion package with a consumer goods producer, briefing a journalist on the appeal of a new facility and so on. The detailed planning and implementation of tasks, the use of marketing tools and the monitoring of the market place requires constant attention and application, a systematic approach which brings greater rewards than a more haphazard management style.

Most of the case studies introduce strategic thrusts either in direct content or implicitly. It is the reader's task to provide a basic strategic framework in almost all instances. The importance of understanding the direction of a company in terms of its corporate aims, marketing objectives and more detailed action plans is essential. Furthermore, being aware of the inter-relationships and overlapping of these different planning levels is equally important. Before attempting any of the case studies it will be worthwhile to look at the introductory comments to Case 1, particularly the summary table of the marketing planning process. A good text to consult is Abell and Hammond.[9]

Segmentation

The marketing task usually begins by understanding the market environment, by identifying market opportunities and provides offerings to meet the requirements of the customers' needs and wants. Once the environment is evaluated then it is important to segment the market and select achievable target groupings. Case 3, The Youth Hostels Association, illustrates how an organisation can segment the market and prepare packages to meet the needs of a particular segment, within the constraints of given resources. Segmentation, of course, depends on the criteria used to divide a market in a viable way, such as by age, socio-economic grouping, life style and stage variables and so on.

Marketing Research

For segmentation to be accurate, the marketeer needs to know about the market in general and about the customer profile for his or her own products. What characteristics do customers share? why do they wish to buy a particular holiday package or visit a certain type of attraction? Small-scale businesses such as guest houses often argue that they are so close to their customers that they have virtually instant feedback about the profiles of their guests and therefore need no formal marketing research activity. Most businesses in the tourism sector are larger and are not able to do this. They need to use more formal market research techniques to find out about their customers, their attitudes, motivations, likes and dislikes. Marketing research is a systematic collection and analysis of data about a market, a product, or competitive offering[10] and is fast becoming accepted as a worthwhile marketing tool by tourism businesses. Case 2, Co-op Travelcare, for example, draws together aspects of marketing research, the distinction between quantitative and qualitative techniques, their value and application.

Once a marketing environment has been analysed, target markets researched and marketing plans made, the marketing task is very much about the application of the marketing mix to the circumstances facing the company or organisation. In service marketing it is suggested that while the traditional mix (Price, Product, Distribution, Promotion) is equally applicable there are a number of definable characteristics which mean that the application of the marketing tools in tourism is different from manufacturing or fast-moving consumer goods. The characteristics are described in Table D and are discussed as they arise in the various case studies.

Product

The core of the marketing mix is the product, a term which is used to incorporate what may be referred to as a service or is sometimes called the service product. The product is the core offering to the customer, the main benefit received by the customer. Aspects of product development and positioning in the market place are raised in Case 4, the Mersey Ferries. In this case, product positioning is crucial. Can a ferry which was once a basic means of transport across the River Mersey be predominantly a leisure pastime now? The case also draws attention to the life cycle concept, as it is very much about the modification to a product in the declining stage of its life cycle.

Table D   The characteristics of service marketing

Characteristic	Example
Intangibility	The customer cannot see tangible evidence of the product being purchased, such as a holiday package
Inseparability	Production and consumption occur at the same time: a guest travelling on a coach tour receives the commentary, the scenery, the pleasant drive as it is being produced
Heterogeneity	Maintaining a consistent product is difficult: the next tour driver might drive in an erratic way, forget to offer a commentary, etc.
Ownership	The consumer does not usually buy the title of goods: i.e. you buy a holiday and take home the dreams (not the resort)
Perishability	The tourism product cannot be stored, unused capacity is lost forever: a hotel with empty rooms cannot stock-pile that capacity for tomorrow

Destination

The concept of the product can be also be viewed in a much wider context when referring to a destination – i.e. a geographical territory with a selection of product offerings such as attractions, shops, seaside, accommodation, etc. – which all make up the 'destination product' or resort offering for the day visitor and staying holidaymaker. Case 8, The English Riviera, discusses the nature of product development and market fit, as well as raising the issues of distinctive branding.

Pricing Strategies

The selection of an appropriate pricing system to meet the needs of a market environment is developed in Case 5, Marches Cycles. Pricing is sometimes confused with costing, and the latter concept tends to dominate approaches to pricing, but there are a variety of approaches which can be utilised at different stages of product or market development. Pricing to greater demand, to alert or to follow competitors, to penetrate or skim the market have to be considered, depending on circumstances.

Promotion

Of all elements of the marketing mix, promotion receives the most attention in tourism, and for many practitioners marketing is perceived as a promotional activity only. Promoting tourism services has become an increasingly complicated task, and marketeers are far more sophisticated in their use of promotional methods. For example, public relations and sponsorship are used, as is database marketing to target groups by mail or telephone.[11] Case 6, Air Miles, allows the reader to assess the importance of using a variety of communication techniques to get the message across to different target groups with different needs. It emphasises the use of sales promotion as a strategic rather than as a tactical marketing tool.

Distribution

Distribution channels are also vital in this communication process. In one sense, distribution is literally seen as access to the destination, attraction, or accommodation. However, it has also to be viewed in a much wider context, in terms of channel management, especially given the rapid improvement of electronic transmission of messages. The development of major global information and computerised booking systems such as Apollo and Sabre in the USA and Amadeus in Europe means that travel agents will be able to access virtually a global booking system. The implications for the market place are important.

One issue which was discussed with vigour during the 1980s was the need, or otherwise, for suppliers of UK products to sell their offerings to the domestic market by way of travel agencies. Case 7, Great British Breaks, not only raises issues about product repositioning and branding but raises the very real problem of getting a product to the market place where it can be easily bought.

Customer Service

In service marketing the 'people dimension' is recognised as being as important as the four traditional marketing mix elements, given that production and consumption of the product generally occur at the same time. This issue of setting standards of service, maintaining consistency and establishing appropriate levels of customer service is a major issue in tourism. The word 'quality' is used very frequently by marketing managers to describe their approach to customers, but how can quality be delivered? This is a major concern of the main hotel groups for it is one of the few ways they can gain – or maintain – a competitive edge in a converging market place. Case 10, Trusthouse Forte, introduces the issue of customer services and quality assurance in the business sector.

International Marketing

Tourism has always been an international business but the growth of this dimension requires a more sophisticated and coordinated approach to the market than most companies in the tourism sector can currently supply. In some instances, multinational organisations are implementing strategies to market their products and operate on a global basis. Several hotel groups now do this and a small number of visitor attractions look to be moving in a similar direction. Most governments are acutely aware of the importance of international tourism, as it affects the balance of payments. They generally have a national tourist office to market their country abroad so as to encourage visitors. The UK is no exception and The British Tourist Authority is charged with this responsibility, albeit on a basis of limited funding. Case 12, The British Tourist Authority, illustrates the way in which an overseas marketing effort is conducted, highlighting the importance of target marketing on a global scale.

Management of Demand

Marketing is also about monitoring and control, about the management of demand. Case 9, Granada Studios Tours, focuses on the issues of seasonality, and how this can be overcome through an imaginative marketing approach. The cyclical nature of demand in terms of the day, week and over an annual cycle presents a great problem for the manager of any attraction. The task becomes more difficult when the attraction is capacity-constrained, as the perishable nature of tourism is well documented. Case 9 introduces the reader to the issues of practical demand management.

Case 11, The Peak District National Park, raises a far wider issue of managing visitors in sensitive areas when visitors are approaching saturation level. The wave of interest in 'Green' tourism is not a temporary phenomenon. The discussion of finite resources and appropriate levels of demand is a matter which is increasingly at the forefront of the tourism marketeer's thinking. Management of demand will be one of the major challenges of the 1990s.

These twelve case studies thus bring to the reader in a very little way the main issues confronting marketeers in the business of tourism.

How to Use the Case Studies

Why Case Studies?

The case studies are listed in Table E. Each case highlights a main issue such as planning in Case 1 or Distribution in Case 7. They also introduce other matters which the marketeer needs to address such as branding, the use of public relations *vis à vis* advertising and so on. The situations are based on live problems which are facing marketing teams in the organisations concerned. More importantly, they are matters which face every marketing executive in tourism at one time or another.

Case studies allow you take a fresh look at a marketing principle and see how it can best be applied to a given situation. Cases also tend to bring out the best in people in terms of analysis. Be analytical in your approach. Where information is not available, make assumptions. Make best estimates of projected outcomes dependent on proposed actions. Most of all, do not be afraid to make decisions on the evidence available for your consideration.

At worst, case studies save you from not being talked at for too long and they often positively instil an interest which drives you to research deeper into the subject area.

Using the Case Studies

The cases can be used in a variety of ways – sometimes for discussion, sometimes to develop your skills in a practical way by writing a report, presenting key findings on an overhead projector or by verbal explanation to colleagues as to how you would handle the assignment. The decision making process is also about team work. Let the discussion flow before reaching conclusions and you will learn from your friends in a collective experience. This discussion is vital, for while marketing is about analysis it is also about the application of creative ideas. Prepare your options and make a decision as to which approach is more appropriate. Equally important, suggest ways in which the decision may be implemented.

Table E   The case studies

	Case	Issues raised
1	The Wales Tourist Board	Planning, Strategy, Branding
2	Co-op Travelcare	Marketing research, Distribution
3	The Youth Hostels Association	Segmentation, Market analysis
4	Mersey Ferries	Product modification, positioning
5	Marches Cycles	Pricing
6	Air Miles	Promotional mix, Actions plans
7	Great British City Breaks	Distribution, Strategy
8	The English Riviera	Marketing destinations, Product development
9	Granada Studios Tours	Seasonality, Quality standards
10	Trusthouse Forte	Customer service, Quality standards
11	The Peak District National Park	Demand management, Environment
12	The British Tourist Authority	Marketing abroad, Sponsorship

It is absolutely essential that you attend the relevant lecture or read the chapter in a tourism marketing text book before you attempt the case studies in this book. Prior knowledge is expected. Only if you have it will you obtain the greatest satisfaction from the cases. Reading suggestions are made at the end of each case. By all means find articles and references in the library relating to the topic in each case, but do not approach the companies and organisations concerned as they have been kind enough to provide the base data for the case studies already. The cases allow analysis and discussion without additional information.

Ensure that you make notes of your findings and at the debriefing sessions. These will be useful if you have to use the material for assignments or in an examination. The cases provide dozens of appropriate examples of tourism marketing applications.

There is no one 'correct' approach in analysing a case, but some may find the following steps a useful guideline:

- read the case briefly
- read it again thoroughly, making a note of the key items

- analyse the data – both the written material and any illustrations
- make a summary statement of the main issues raised by the case
- set out a series of questions, and reply to them with written answers
- answer as accurately as you can the questions asked of you, and in the format requested

When it comes to cases, the author or examiner is often seeking a framework for an answer, possible solutions, or recommendations. Do not be afraid to make assumptions where vital pieces of information are missing. Marketeers in tourism have to do this all the time. The lecturer or examiner will be looking to see whether you can analyse the written and numerical content, apply theory to applied situations and, lastly, communicate your analysis and decisions in a relevant way.

Do not necessarily read the introductory notes in each case first. Sometimes, it is better to take a look at the case/problem and define the issues as you see them. Then, write down what you consider to be the main questions to ask or the key tasks to fulfil. Complete these first and then return to the notes or the tasks suggested in the book.

The accompanying notes should, however, provide a useful review of the area being discussed. They can be read separately as an introduction to the subject matter before reading additional material to enrich your current understanding.

Whichever way you intend to use the book, positive and clear thinking counts!

References

1. A. Jefferson and L. Lickorish, *Marketing Tourism: A Practical Guide* (Longman, 1988).
2. R.C. Mill and A.M. Morrison, *The Tourism System: An Introductory Text* (Prentice-Hall International, 1985).
3. A.J. Burkart and S. Medlik, *Tourism Past, Present and Future*, 2nd edn (Heinemann, 1981).
4. J.C. Holloway and R.V. Plant, *Marketing For Tourism* (Pitman, 1988).
5. V.T.C. Middleton, *Marketing in Travel and Tourism* (Heinemann, 1988).
6. The Tourism Society, *Handbook*/1979.
7. Middleton, *Marketing in Travel and Tourism*.
8. M. Martin, 'Tourism Marketing Management', in S.F. Witt and L. Moutinho (eds), *Tourism Marketing and Management Handbook* (Prentice-Hall, 1989).

9. D.F. Abell and J.S. Hammond, *Strategic Market Planning* (Prentice-Hall, 1979).
10. S. Crouch, *Marketing Research for Managers* (Heinemann, 1984).
11. F. Moyle, 'English Tourism: Facing up to the big push?', *Marketing Week* (13 October 1989).

1 The Wales Tourist Board: Rural Tourism Initiative

BWRDD CROESO CYMRU
WALES TOURIST BOARD

Objectives

(a) To understand the marketing planning process
(b) To evaluate new product development

Marketing Planning

Planning of any business activity is vital if there is to be a sense of direction and an effective use of the organisation's resources. Whether it be a National Tourist Board or a visitor attraction the ability to organise the marketing effort more effectively and to control the process through monitoring, diagnosis and modification is a stabilising force in an environment of change. Planning need not be a stultifying process; it should allow coordination and flexibility. The overall planning process is described admirably by McDonald[1] and also by Baker[2] although in a tourism context the reader might prefer Middleton[3] or Jefferson and Lickorish[4]. Table 1.1 outlines the main process as applied to tourism marketing.

The term 'strategy', derived from military terminology, relates to the way in which an organisation seeks to meet its objectives and usually refers to the main lines of direction, statements which explain how things are made to happen over a given timescale. Confusion often arises as strategies may sometimes be set out as tactical or as action plans – i.e. a more detailed account of how things will work.

Table 1.1   The marketing planning process – tourism

Corporate objectives
Example:
A Hotel Group's Board sets a goal of being the largest hotel group in the world by the year 2000

Marketing audit/
Thorough review, positional statement about internal, external environment – i.e. political unrest in the Middle East stops development/threat to global policy

Swot analysis
Includes a strengths, weaknesses, opportunities, threats analysis, but analysis must be wider and deeper
Examples:
Strength: Management and staff might be well trained
Weakness: Poor sales staff in USA
Opportunity: Hotels for sale in Germany
Threat: Another hotel group is emerging faster than expected

Objectives
This brings a reappraisal of existing objectives – for example, the increase in profits by 8 per cent in one year, acquisition of 100 hotels in Australia in 2 years

Strategies
Major approaches to making the objectives successful – for example, establish a strategic development group to source new hotels, sell a new accommodation package to businesses globally
Process involves analysis, choice and implementation

Programmes of work/short-range or tactical plans
Implement chosen strategies and mixes, prioritise, schedule, budget and execute details
Six-month tactical campaign to promote new hotel features, sometimes involving contingency measures dependent on competitor reaction

Monitoring
Should be continuous and built in to the above stages
Control should also feature strongly throughout – budgetary, time and resource control

Note that the terminology for each respective planning activity differs in text books, but the general sequence of the planning tasks is almost universal.

There is no 'correct' approach, but for purposes of clarity it is best to adopt a format that draws a distinction between objectives and strategy, and then goes on to consider action programmes and monitoring/control.

Objectives – What an organisation wishes to achieve within a given time-scale, preferably expressed in a quantified manner: for example, a company could seek to increase its market share by 5 per cent during the next twelve months

Strategy – This outlines in 'broad brush' terms how an organisation is going to achieve its objectives; this requires strategy formulation – an assessment of all available information, the setting out of possible options and strategic implementation

Action programmes (or tactical plans) – These documents set out how the above mentioned strategies are going to work in detail. They specify actions and how they are to be made to happen, who will supply the finance, the marketing skills, etc., and when

Monitoring and control – Measures for assessing the effectiveness of the strategy have to be built into the process

---

If a company wishes to incorporate detail into a strategic document this is no bad thing if the main approaches can still be readily identified. Sometimes, however, strategies become cluttered with detail and the main thrusts, such as market penetration or diversification, are lost in the overall detail. Main planks of strategy should be made boldly in strategic or executive summaries at the beginning of a document setting out an organisation's marketing strategy.

In the tourism sector, planning documents appear in all shapes and sizes. When it comes to a major visitor attraction or hotel group the planning format might well take a formal approach and is often embodied in a document known as the 'Marketing Plan', possibly spanning three or five years but sometimes one year only. This plan should be cross-referenced to a Corporate plan, a goal-orientated document outlining 'scenarios' of where the company wishes to be in the longer term. A major international hotel group such as Hilton International or Holiday Inn might thus prepare a corporate plan which stated the company's key intentions in a global setting over the coming 20 to 25 years. From this all other planning documents should flow, such as the three-year marketing plan, or short-term plans spanning three–six months, etc. They should all be inextricably linked to the corporate plan, not forgetting the wider aims and direction of the company.

When it comes tourism planning in a geographical context, planning documents tend to be of a different nature as they have to encompass all aspects of development such as optimum levels of accommodation, types of attractions, access,etc. They also tend to be less emphatic in terms of achievements which can brought to fruition in a given timescale. This is hardly surprising as those responsible for carrying out the actions vary from the Department of Transport and British Rail, to voluntary tourism associations and private consortia. All manner of companies and organisations will be involved in terms of preparation, strategic content and implementation. The more parties concerned, the more fragmented the process is likely to be. Thus, while marketing plans or strategic plans prepared by Tourist Boards and tourist authorities are rigorous in approach they do not necessarily enable the authority to do more than coordinate or advise the marketing approach of a group of suppliers. Resourcing then becomes a crucial issue.

In recent years in England much tourism planning and strategy work at a local and regional level has developed under the banner of the Tourism Development Action Programmes (TDAP) which follow a sequence of marketing audit, outline plan, and then a programme for action over a three-year period. These initiatives have been very successful in stimulating partnerships between public and private sector providers to market an area successfully, consultation bringing those interested into the process into a joint planning exercise.

At a national level, the English Tourist Board's marketing plan was originally set out in *A Vision For England*[5]. This was revised with a consultative document outlining strategy for the 1990s.[6]

In Scotland and Wales a similar process has been undertaken with the boards preparing major strategy documents. The Wales Tourist Board, 'Tourism in Wales . . . Developing the Potential'[7], prepared following consultation with local authorities and trade interests, set out a strategy for the early 1990s. Case 1 relates to part of this overall strategy, The Rural Tourism Initiative.

The Case

The Wales Tourist Board was established in 1969 under the Development of Tourism Act alongside the other national and regional Tourist Boards and the British Tourist Authority. It has a statutory duty to promote tourism to and within Wales, to encourage and assist the provision of tourist facilities and amenities in Wales and to advise government, local authorities and other agencies on tourism matters. The Wales Tourist Board corporate policy objectives (see Figure 1.1) highlight the importance of the need to promote Welsh culture, language

Figure 1.1   Wales Tourist Board: objectives

The Objectives of the Board

1.7   The Board re-affirms the ten corporate policy
objectives listed below which together underpin
its development and marketing activities.
Implicit in each of these objectives is the need
to sustain and promote Welsh culture, language
and heritage, to protect and enhance the
physical environment of Wales, and to ensure
the economic and social well-being of the host
community:-

i)   to promote Wales as an attractive
      destination for all forms of tourism and
      day visits throughout the year;

ii)   to facilitate the marketing efforts of the
      tourist industry, both public and private
      sectors;

iii) to encourage investment in the
      improvement and development of all
      forms of tourist accommodation;

iv)   to encourage investment and
      improvement of all forms of tourist and
      visitor attractions and other facilities,
      including infrastructure provision where
      necessary;

v)   to encourage the development and
      promotion of specific events designed for
      tourists and day visitors;

vi)   to encourage the provision of tourist
      information, quality controls and other
      means of securing visitors satisfaction
      within Wales;

vii) to encourage education and training
      facilities for employees in the Welsh
      tourist industry;

viii) to assist developers and operators within
      the tourism industry in Wales through
      advisory services;

ix)   to inspire and work with all other
      organisations whose activities can help
      promote the tourism industry in Wales;

x)   to effectively convey the importance of the
      tourism industry to the Welsh economy
      and the objectives and work of the Board
      to the operators in the industry, local and
      central government, other interested
      organisations and to the public at large.

Source: Wales Tourist Board.

and heritage, to protect and enhance the physical environment of Wales and to ensure the economic and social well-being of the host community – i.e. safeguarding the very aspects which make it such an attractive destination.

These statements could not be more appropriate when one considers the background data. Wales is one-seventh the size of England and has a population of only 2.8 million, concentrated mainly in the populated areas of the South East of Wales or the North Wales coast. The remainder is predominantly rural with very low levels of population settled along its dramatic coastline, in the uplands and in the valleys beneath magnificent mountain scenery. Figures 1.2 and 1.3 provide the reader with an indication of the scale and scope of tourism in Wales.

The Wales Tourist Board, in taking stock of what Wales had to offer earlier in the 1980s, reviewed the comparative strengths and weaknesses in general terms. These are listed in Figure 1.4. The Board also investigated general market trends in the UK, with the following conclusions:

- Growth in the 25–34 age group by 12 per cent
- A 6 per cent rise in the 45–59 and 60+ age groups
- Domestic expenditure and time spent on enjoyment of leisure will increase as well as an interest in learning, active pursuits and widening experience
- According to BTA forecasts there will be a growth of overseas visitors of 4 per cent between 1988 and 1992 including an increasing dispersal from London
  The number of short breaks is estimated to increase by 10 per cent
- Day trips are likely to increase, albeit at a slower rate
- Relative decline has been predicted in the 15–19 age group(–19 per cent) and to a lesser extent the 20–24 age group (–7 per cent)
- The traditional long-stay holiday of 4+ nights is still in decline despite a halt to the rapid growth of overseas package holidays

---

The Board, following extensive consultation with several sections of the tourism business at regional and local level felt there was a strong case for launching a new initiative on behalf of rural tourism in the late 1980s. Previous research[8] had indicated that the appeal of Wales within the UK was strongly associated with its very varied and beautiful countryside. The basic core product, the landscape, the farming communities, people in villages, rural attractions such as walking routes, old mills and houses were thus already in situ and simply required good husbandry and conservation. However, there was no real strategy to pull

Figure 1.2   The scale of tourism in Wales: tourist expenditure

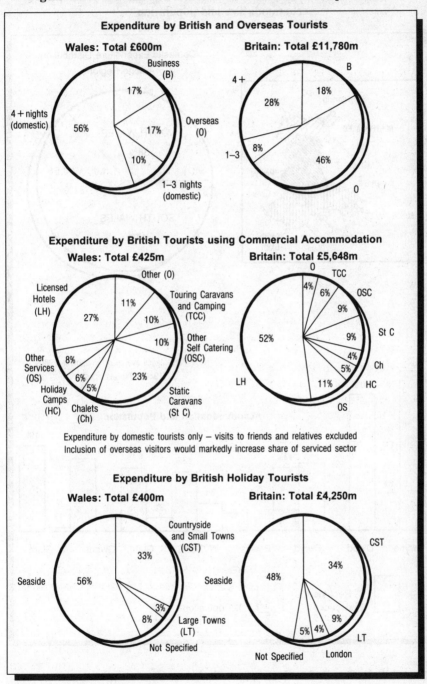

Source: Wales Tourist Board.

Figure 1.3   The scale of tourism in Wales: expenditure distribution, accommodation and population

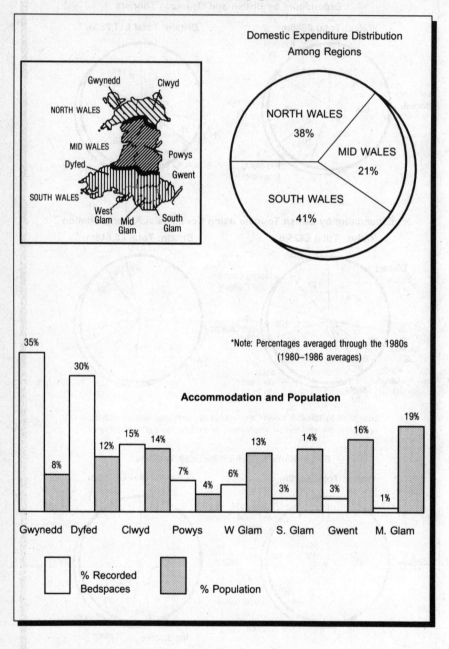

Source: Wales Tourist Board.

Figure 1.4 Resource assets, constraints and potential

1. ASSETS
    Physical environment:
    scenic qualities of mountains, hills, valleys and
    coasts, beaches and inland waters,
    peace and quiet

    Human and built environment:
    distinctive language, heritage and culture
    warmth of welcome generally enjoyed
    castles and historic buildings
    industrial heritage
    scenic railways
    Victorian resorts

    Tourism Infrastructure:
    wide range of accommodation and attractions
    well established resorts
    countryside activity opportunities
    proximity to major domestic markets
    established tourism information services
    receptive tourism development agencies

2. CONSTRAINTS
    Physical environment:
    unpredictable summer weather
    quality of bathing waters

    Human and built environment:
    negative images of unfriendly people
    negative images of industrial dereliction
    negative images of down market poor
    quality products
    unattractive parts of some towns and villages

    Tourism infrastructure:
    existence of significant elements of shabby,
    outmoded, poor quality provision in all sectors of tourism
    capacity deficiencies in some accommodation sectors
    relatively poor provision of all-weather facilities

3. POTENTIAL FOR IMPROVEMENT
    Enjoyable range of visitor attractions
    Heritage interpretation
    Speciality shopping
    Accommodation quality
    Some new accommodation provision
    Network of group travel hotels
    Canal boats holidays
    Use of inland water areas
    Catering standards
    Business exhibition facilities
    Entrepreneurial confidence
    Operator professionalism
    Marketable development sites
    Signposting
    Stimulation of civic and community pride

Source: Wales Tourist Board.

these aspects together in terms of distinct products which could be purchased by potential visitors, a strategy which would focus on accommodation stock. Furthermore, how it could be brought to the market in an attractive manner? The Rural Tourism Initiative thus began to be discussed in detail.

The objectives of the new initiative were as follows;

1. To establish a strong, distinctive image for Wales rural tourism destinations, in selected UK markets, through the development of well-defined products with unique selling propositions
2. To develop new business and increase the profitability of existing tour operators
3. To encourage the establishment of new tourism operators
4. To encourage improvements in the quality of accommodation standards, and in the range and quality of tourist facilities and services in rural Wales

The Task

As an executive working on the initiative you have been asked to draw up a strategy for meeting these objectives. It should outline
(a) Possible products, including ways in which product enhancement can be introduced and branding identified
(b) Suitable markets for the product offerings

References

1. M. H. B. McDonald, *Marketing Plans: How to Prepare Them How to Use Them* (Heinemann, 1989).
2. M. J. Baker, *Marketing Planning and Strategy* (Macmillan, 1985).
3. V. T. C. Middleton, *Marketing in Travel and Tourism* (Heinemann, 1988).
4. A. Jefferson and L. Lickorish, *Marketing Tourism: A Practical Guide* (Longman, 1988)
5. English Tourist Board, *A Vision For England* (ETB, 1988).

6. English Tourism Board, *Tourism Towards The Year 2000: A New Strategy For England* (ETB Consultative Document, 1990).
7. Wales Tourist Board, *Tourism In Wales: Developing The Potential* (WTB, 1988).
8. Wales Tourist Board, *Attitudes to Wales as a Tourist Destination* (WTB, 1985).

The author gratefully acknowledges the assistance of The Wales Tourist Board in the preparation of this case. Certain aspects have been amended to maintain confidentiality of data.

2 Co-op Travelcare: Retailing in the 1990s

Objectives

(a) To introduce travel retailing
(b) To evaluate qualitative marketing research methods

Distribution Channels

Distribution channels can often make or break a product in tourism as in any other business. In terms of the UK domestic products, holidays and other travel packages are usually sold direct to the customer by the supplier and this is common, for example, with offerings such as holiday cottages or activity breaks. The overseas package holiday market is different. Holidays are generally sold by way of intermediaries on behalf of the major tour operators bringing together packages. Some tour operators, however, such as Tjaereborg and Portland Holidays, for example, deal almost exclusively by selling direct. Nevertheless, most packaged holidays are still sold by way of retail outlets, the retail travel agency network.

Retail Travel Agencies

There are approximately 7500 High Street travel agency outlets in Britain offering a vast range of products to the potential customer. Their importance grew in the 1970s with improved availability of cheaper package holidays to Mediterranean resorts. The push came mainly from the main tour operators Clarksons and Thomson. Subsequent growth in the number of retail agencies has been dramatic, a rise from around 4000 in 1977 to nearly 7000 in 1987, although the growth has since stopped. The characteristic of the business has always been a world of small independents, as illustrated in Figure 2.1. Since the early 1980s, however, there has been an increase in the large multiples such as Lunn Poly, Thomas Cook and Pickfords and consolidation in the market continues in the 1990s (see Figure 2.2).

Figure 2.1   Multiple travel agents, 1984 and 1989

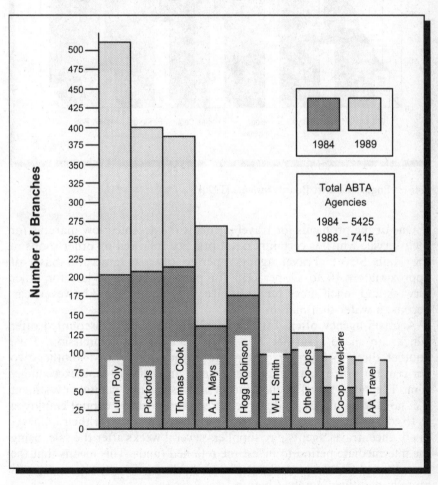

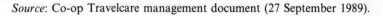
Source: Co-op Travelcare management document (27 September 1989).

Figure 2.2   Rapid growth of mega-multiples, 1982–9

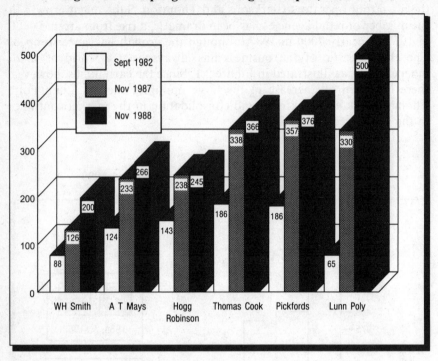

Source: English Tourist Board, *Insights* (1990).

One of the problems for travel agents is the accepted low margins for their service which is certainly not a practice followed by other shops in the High Street. Travel agents operate on a commission basis of approximately 10 to 11 per cent for package holidays, less for other services and much more for insurance. This commission, however, can become a wafer-thin margin.

A travel agency often, for example, bears a special discounted offer which can shave a further 2 to 3 per cent off the commission. Take another three to four per cent off to cover staffing, and another two per cent for office costs and the gross margin begins to look exceedingly slim. The retail travel agency business lives on low capital investment (i.e. no stockpiling of products required) and negative capital employed as fixed capital is financed by creditors. Customers pay for their holidays in advance, travel agents pay suppliers several weeks after the sale, using the intermediate period to invest the retained funds. This means that the pressure on travel agents to perform in terms of customer volume is more imperative than ever before.

At the same time tour operation has become dominated by a small number of suppliers. Thomson is decidedly the market leader, having

taken over Horizon in the mid-1980s. The supply position has consolidated further with the collapse of Intasun in 1991 and thus the existing
tour operators have more sway with the retail chains than ever before.
Furthermore with the dramatic improvement of electronically transmit-
ted information systems they can sell as easily from their computerised
inventory of holidays to the customer as to a travel agency, hence saving
the intermediary fee.

The importance of location for a travel agency is, therefore, para-
mount and establishing customer credibility equally so. The design of
retail outlets to present the right 'feel' and the value of staff are all issues
which marketing and retail managers have to consider very carefully,
given the competitive environment.

Marketing Research

Marketing research plays a very important part in the distribution
process and is essential for tour operators and travel agents alike. The
latter have a need to research why customers prefer some locations to
others, what attracts them to the shop, what they like and dislike about
the shop, what they think about their levels of service *vis à vis* other
agencies and so on. The range of market research opportunites are
summarised in Table 2.1.

Quantitative techniques are sometimes used to gather data about
customers. For example, most of the major tour operators issue package
holiday travellers with a questionnaire on the flight home. On the plane
the customer has time to reflect and time to fill in a fairly lengthy form.
Thus, a mass of data is collected on a continuous basis about the travel,
destination resort, hotels, apartments and hotels visited by the customer.
This type of survey, where the interviewee has to interpret the question
and provide a 'gut' response has to be structured in approach. A
respondent might thus be asked whether he or she thought the flight
was very good, good, satisfactory, poor and very poor by ticking the
appropriate box. Aggregate opinion trends can then be collated and
assessed. The results however, do not begin to tell us why the holiday was
booked, or whether the customer is loyal or not.

Qualitative techniques are more appropriate for delving into reasons
why people prefer certain aspects of one shop or hotel to another, into
their habits, their perceptions and values. The techniques are not
statistically verifiable as, say, a random sample (see Figure 2.3) of every
20th customer coming into the travel agency would be, but they do
provide an insight into how the customer thinks and behaves. There are
several reference texts for the reader wishing to read more about market
research methodologies available, such as Middleton,[1] Chisnall[2] and
Worcester.[3]

Table 2.1   Marketing research methods summary

Desk research
Review of secondary data
Use of reports such as the English Tourist Board *Insights* to check
trends, etc., or through company reports which are packed with data

Primary research
Quantitative
Continuous monitoring: Very often used by major attractions to
monitor flows of customers, exit surveys to assess satifaction levels
On a world or national basis surveys such as the International
Passenger Survey provide data about flows of tourist, or the British
Tourism Survey on a monthly basis
Regular surveys: These are usually carried out on a quarterly or
annual basis on behalf of the regional or national tourist board,
such as the Holiday Intentions Survey, where a sample of the
population are asked several questions about their intended main
and secondary holidays
Ad hoc surveys: These are usually structured interviews of visitors to
an area or customers of a company, with a view to assessing one or
more particular aspects – thus, a local authority might wish to find
out what visitors tend to do at a country park, or a hotel what guests
think about a new in-house health centre
Omnibus: This is where a company or tourist board buys a
question(s) alongside other companies on a structured questionnaire – thus, an activity breaks company might not have the
resources to find out attitudes to activity breaks among families
with older children in Scandinavia, so seeks this approach as the
next best avenue
Syndicated: Research is carried out in the market about a specified
topic by a market research agency and then it is sold in report or
briefing form to interested parties – Keynote or the *Economist*
Intelligence unit produce several reports from updates on what is
happening in the restaurant business to trends in the long-haul
holiday market
Qualitative
Delphi Techniques: Opinion leaders in the tourism sector are
sometimes asked independently about future trends, and then
having made a prediction are exposed to the views of others on
the panel to see if there is any movement of projected trends;
consultancies sometimes use this technique
Panel or group discussions: Selected groups of people are gathered
together to discuss collectively views about a service, a new

development, a design or an advert; this is often used in new product development

Observation techniques: in menu planning, designing a passenger reception area, etc. observation techniques or tastings are sometimes arranged, as are eye-scan techniques for advertisement responses

The Case

Co-op Travelcare is the seventh largest chain of retail travel agencies, with 90 outlets throughout the country and a concentration of shops in the North West and South East of England. The parent company, The Co-operative Wholesale Society Ltd (CWS) has its headquarters in Manchester and has been involved in tour operation and travel retailing since 1905, first providing packages for its own employees and later for others. In 1946, the Excursions department became known as the Co-operative Travel Service (CWS Ltd) and pioneered the provision of continental holidays. It was one of the first to charter aircraft for package holidays under the brand 'Sun Flight Holidays', and was the first operator to introduce uniformed hostesses in continental resorts during the early 1950s.

Figure 2.3 Sampling in marketing research

Sampling is a method where market researchers attempt to find out about a large group, known as the population, by way of looking at a much smaller part of it, a sample. The concern is to ensure that the sample is representative of the population as a whole. Sampling plans (setting up a sample frame) fall into two main categories:

Probability samples
● Simple random sampling
Simple random sampling is a method used to remove sampling bias. It may be defined as a process of selection whereby each of the population's units has a calculable probability of being selected. Two methods of selection are commonly used – the lottery method and the use of random numbers. Therefore, the sampling error can be calculated (i.e. the likelihood of the sampling not being representative of the population)

- Stratified sampling
The population is segmented into homogeneous layers and a random sample of each is taken
- Cluster sampling
The population is divided into different groups, very often on a geographical basis, and a random sample of each of these groups is undertaken

Non-probability samples
These do not involve random sampling techniques. For example, quota sampling involves the interviewer choosing respondents such as visitors to an attraction over the age of 50, etc.

With the growth of demand for travel during the 1960s, both the retail and tour operation aspects of the business grew and travel agencies were established in Co-operative Retail Society stores throughout the country. In 1971 the retail side of the business became known as Co-op Travel and the tour operation Own Brand Holidays. Further rationalisation took place in 1978 when the CWS established a Travel and Hotels Group to manage both the retail travel business and Travco Hotels, another CWS subsidiary. The merger was intended to strengthen the latter's position in the ailing UK long-stay holiday market.

Travco Hotels continued to sustain losses and given that many of the hotels were in need of considerable refurbishment they were sold in 1983 and 1984. At the same time, the policy of operating retail travel agencies within stores was being reappraised, as returns in many outlets were not acceptable. Thus, a number of in-store outlets were sold to local Co-operative Retail Societies and in their place Co-op Travel opened High Street outlets. In 1983 a Manchester-based chain of travel agents, Stantons, was purchased and in 1985 the Royal Arsenal Co-operative Society released 21 retail outlets to Co-op Travel.

Thus, by 1985 the CWS Travel Group comprised 55 branches, 276 staff and created a turnover of £33.38 million, a figure which had in real terms fluctuated little during the early 1980s. The CWS Travel Group traded in the High Street under 14 different names and this proved to be confusing for staff, suppliers and customers.

In 1985, The Travel Group was reorganised and a new management team introduced to set out a survival strategy for the Group in a highly competitive business environment, as shown in Figure 2.4. Figure 2.5 outlines the structure of the management team, which proved to be very effective given worsening trading conditions in 1988 and 1989. During 1989 Co-op Travelcare acquired Badger Travel, further improving the productivity of the entire Travel Group and providing a wider range of outlets, particularly in the South of England. Figure 2.1 indicates the size of multiple travel agents as at September 1989.

Figure 2.4 Travel group strategy 1985–1989

- Create a strong, attractive retail identity
- Raise standards of facilities and staff
- Computerise branch control systems and reduce central costs to under 1 per cent
- Develop high profile in the media and trade
- Introduce discounting where appropriate
- Seek new business opportunities and associations
- Generate acceptable profits
- Increase profitable market share

Source: Co-op Travelcare.

The management team argued that it was imperative to adopt a new corporate identity and to redesign and refurbish shops to meet customer expectations. A marketing research agency was briefed regarding these matters, with a subsequent change of name to Co-op Travelcare and a programme of redesign and refurbishment of shops. The overall approach brought about a steadily improving market share and profitability without the need for direct discounting. One succesful inducement to the customer was the offer of subsidised travel to a local airport, and this was followed by a 'Nil Deposit' campaign for early bookers. Both cost little to implement in contrast to the increase in value perceived by the customer.

Furthermore, it was obvious to management that investment in training was paying off as Co-op Travel Care was winning increased numbers of late bookings in comparison to other multiples, thought to be a result of professional window displays and stronger selling skills of staff.

The need to continue to update and improve the corporate image was also important and in 1989 Co-op Travelcare decided to conduct further market research to build on the data provided in 1986. This was to be incorporated into a report outlining the future of Co-op Travelcare for the coming three years. The brief to the chosen market research agency simply asked for a review of consumer perceptions of Co-op Travelcare in its market context.

Figure 2.5   Structure of Management team

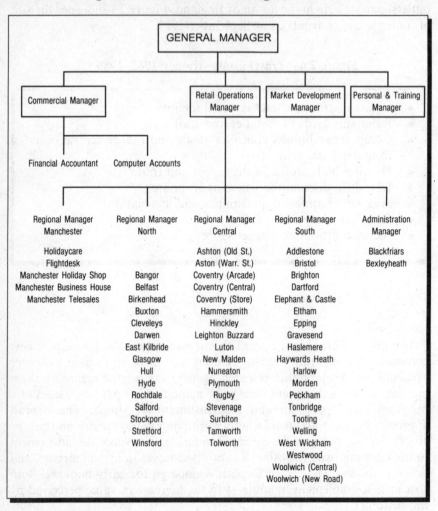

Source: Co-op Travelcare management document (27 September 1989).

The Task

As a research executive with the marketing research agency, you are responsible for progressing the project. Restate the brief in terms of research objectives and explain the methodology you would use to meet these objectives, including the major questions to be asked and what limitations could be anticipated with your approach.

References

1. V.T.C. Middleton *Marketing in Travel and Tourism* (Heinemann, 1988).
2. P. Chisnall, *Marketing Research*, 3rd edn (McGraw Hill, 1987).
3. R. Worcester and J. Downham, *Consumer Marketing Research Handbook*, 3rd edn (McGraw Hill, 1986).

The author gratefully acknowledges the assistance of Co-op Travelcare in the preparation of this case. Certain aspects have been amended to maintain confidentiality of data.

3 The Youth Hostels Association: Great Escapes

Objectives

(a) Understand the meaning of segmentation and target marketing
(b) Introduce market analysis

Segmenting the Market

Market segmentation is a crucial concept to the marketeer, for there are very few companies who seek to woo the entire population. The likelihood is that not all people will be interested in nor want to purchase, their offering. The total market for tourism-related services thus tends to be segmented into sub-groups which become far more achievable targets. For example, an up-market country hotel and golf club might decide to concentrate on corporate hospitality clients and market to companies only. Legoland in Denmark, on the other hand, targets mainly young families from Northern Europe.

This case study emphasises the importance of market segmentation, but also illustrates how marketing tools can be used effectively for organisations, such as the Youth Hostels Association (England and Wales), which have different corporate goals from those of the traditional public limited company.

Marketeers suggest, however, that it is important to ensure that a segment is accurately defined. Kotler,[1] for example, suggests four main criteria which ensure that a segment can be used effectively for targeting. The segment should be

(a) **Measurable** – so that the size and purchasing capability of the group can be assessed.
(b) **Accessible** – The segments must be able to be effectively reached
(c) **Substantial** – The segments have to be large enough to be worth pursuing for commercial return
(d) **Actionable** – The degree to which a company can appropriately target a segment given resource levels

Chisnal[2] and Middleton[3] also discuss the importance of viability and appropriateness.

There are numerous ways in which a market can be segmented, as outlined in Tables 3.1–3.3. In terms of tourism most companies tend to segment according to age, gender, socio-economic grouping, life cycle and geographical dispersion, referred to by Kotler[4] as multivariable analysis. Thus, for example, a farmhouse bed and breakfast group in Scotland might target middle-aged 'empty-nesters' in professional or administrative jobs who have a predisposition for the countryside and happen to live within a three-hour drive time away from their location.

Once a segment can be identified and data exist about a group of customers, it is possible to target accordingly. Many tourism concerns segment their market successfully into a variety of potential customers and transmit different appeals to each segment accordingly. A hotel will, for example, highlight back-up facilities and attention to detail to conference organisers, a welcome reception and light entertainment to a coach party and a warm fireside scene to couples in search of a quiet weekend. Visitor attractions do the same. Their approach to the family market is far lighter in content and style than the educational kit sent to teachers wishing to bring a party of youngsters.

Target Marketing

Nevertheless, one of the successes of marketing in tourism during the 1980s was the increasingly sophisticated approach to targeting by way of identifying clearly the segments likely to show potential. Segmentation has also allowed the organisation to position itself more accurately. A cheese-making dairy open to the public might appeal to discerning consumers with disposable income to buy a quality product, who have an interest in healthy food and rural ways of life and who are looking to while away an interesting hour or so before buying some of the products to take home. The farm's promotional appeal can convey these messages. On the other hand, a theme park attracting families and parties of young people projects itself as offering non-stop fun, plenty of heart-thumping, stomach-curdling thrills and a thoroughly good day out in a happy atmosphere. The theme park's positioning in the attractions market is therefore quite different, with a price-sensitive offering and cheerful promotion to encourage mass business. Targeting is fundamental to effective marketing.

The Case

The Youth Hostels Association (England and Wales) was established in 1930 with the following object:

> To help all, especially young people of limited means, to a greater knowledge, love and care of the countryside, particularly by providing hostels or other simple accommodation for them in their travels; and thus to promote their health, rest and education.

The YHA therefore has a very different business mission from most organisations engaged in providing accommodation and package holidays in the UK. The major policy directions of the Youth Hostels Association (England and Wales) are made by a National Executive Committee, comprising a mixture of voluntary members and employed executives. The execution of policy is undertaken by The Chief Executive and paid staff employed within the following functional areas:

- Marketing
- Operations
- Personnel
- Finance

In terms of operation, England and Wales is divided into five regions, each controlled by a Regional Director and a small support staff. The regions are:

- Northern England
- Central England
- South of England
- Wales
- London

There are 258 youth hostels providing accommodation in bunk-bedded dormitories of various sizes and there are family rooms at some locations. There are other facilities such as kitchens where the guest can prepare a meal, a dining room, amenities area, drying rooms and toilet/shower blocks. Youth hostels are mainly situated in rural areas but some are based in towns. They tend to be characterful buildings such as Wilderhope Manor, St Bravial's Castle, or Beverley Friary.

Youth hostels are generally closed during the daytime, have set times for meals, request that members staying assist with minor tasks in running the establishment and have a 'doors closed' time and a 'lights out' ruling at night time. This is seen as commensurate with the overall objectives of the Association and helping with the chores helps to keep prices down. There is some consumer resistance to this so that many rules have been relaxed, but the 'community atmosphere' is in fact seen as one of the benefits of youth hostelling.

The facilities vary enormously from very basic provision in remote areas to superior hostels more akin to hotel provision. The stock of accommodation is a great strength to the YHA, but also a threat in that the maintenance, upkeep and upgrading of so many historic buildings draws heavily on the surplus made in trading activities. The development of the YHA stock is of prime importance. There is a considerable refurbishment programme of older properties taking place, and new hostels have recently been built in pleasant cities such as Bristol and York

Every youth hostel is managed by a warden providing in most cases accommodation, meals and a small retail outlet. Other facilities are provided, such as cycle hire, outdoor pursuits, tuition and equipment, for example. Table 3.1 illustrates the supply of youth hostels in England and Wales since the Association began, and the sale of overnight accommodation.

Use of youth hostels is for members of the YHA only, and thus one of the key marketing tasks is to increase membership. The categories of membership are shown in Table 3.2.

The market for accommodation and related outdoor activities comprises three main segments, the main marketing task being to encourage those segments to use youth hostels as much as possible especially where capacity exists.

Table 3.1   Hostels and overnight stays

Year	Members	Hostels	Beds	Overnights
1931	6439	73	1562	–
1935	48057	239	6398	307811
1940	50864	236	8267	275600
1945	153751	234	9595	746699
1950	210142	303	13971	1157802
1955	186796	286	13912	1041823
1960	181958	270	13385	1096880
1965	219336	271	13573	1239679
1970	234621	259	13202	1453776
1975	274992	264	13973	1843989
1980	309341	277	15383	1940199
1981	281132	282	15858	1789719
1982	257258	284	15661	1679105
1983	255246	278	15372	1721006
1984	251550	270	15045	1793974
1985	255261	260	14707	1871033
1986	269914	254	14553	1808440
1987	274849	275	15205	1977340
1988	286635	261	15052	2078071
1989	314093	258	15090	2150271

Source: Youth Hostels Association (England and Wales) *Annual Report*, 1989

Table 3.2   Categories of membership

Membership	As at 30.09.88	As at 30.09.89	As at 30.09.90
Young (0–15)	37074	39549	38351
Junior (16–21)	67952	76074	76450
Senior (21+)	181609	198470	205946
Total	286635	314093	320747

Source: Youth Hostels Association (England and Wales) Annual Report 1989 and Marketing Section

Foreign visitors – The YHA belongs to an international movement of similar organisations throughout the world, known as the International Youth Hostels Federation. This encourages young people to visit other parts of the world in order to widen horizons, understand other cultures and meet others from different countries. England and Wales receives a large number of overseas members.
Individual Members – England and Wales members travelling on their own or in small groups.
Groups – Organised party bookings either by existing YHA local groups and other parties, mainly school groups.

Table 3.3 shows the distribution of overnight usage between these three segments during the years 1986–9.

Table 3.3 Overnight usage

Proportion of total overnights recorded by	1986	(%)	1987	(%)	1988	(%)	1989	(%)
Foreign								
visitors	545664	30.2	606481	30.7	647064	31.1	684360	31.8
members	851650	47.1	892530	45.1	854280	41.1	888353	41.3
groups	411126	22.7	478329	24.2	576727	27.8	577558	26.9
Total	1808440	100	1977340	100	2078071	100	2150271	100

Source: Youth Hostels Association (England and Wales) *Annual Report* 1989.

In 1986 it was decided that one way to keep pace with contemporary young people was to develop a package of activity-based holidays which has since been branded 'Great Escapes'. At the same time a similar range of holidays had been devised, known as 'Leisure Breaks', for those wishing to pursue an interest of shorter duration but not necessarily an activity such as sailing or climbing.

The Great Escapes packages provide the following, or a combination of the respective activities:

Watersports – Multi-Watersports, Canoeing, Sailing, Sub-Aqua, Windsurfing
Airsports – Multi-Airsports, Hang Gliding, Gliding, Paragliding, Parachuting
Walking and Cycling – Hill Walking, Cycle Tour
Mountain Sports – Caving, Climbing, Cross Country Skiing, Mountaineering
Riding and Biking – Horse Riding, Mountain Biking
Young Adventure – From Canoeing to Pony Riding but for an age range 12–15

Two youth hostels at Edale and Llangollen were refurbished and developed as Multi-Activity holiday centres with a purpose of being flagships for the overall product and thirty other youth hostels throughout England and Wales were incorporated into the promotion. The YHA marketing department were very keen to use Great Escapes as a way of attracting new members and establishing the YHA firmly in the activity market. The market is likely to become more aggressive in the coming years, given the population trends for the key market segment (see Table 3.4) but the buoyant short breaks market overall shows promise (see Figure 3.1).

The Great Escapes package has done moderately well given the limited budget devoted to the campaign. The Marketing Director, however, felt that the brochure, of which 350,000 were being produced and 280,000 despatched to members, had to signal more immediately the core offering of the product to young people. She felt that the impact of adventure and excitement in taking part in multi-outdoor activities with people of a similar age was the key message to get across, visually and in the copy. Furthermore, she had had an opportunity to reappraise a limited survey of existing Great Escapes users, as shown in Table 3.5 which provided an idea of how the product was being received.

The Task

As a research student, you have approached the Youth Hostels Association(England and Wales) with a view to preparing a marketing analysis of the youth activity holidays market. You also wish to suggest ways in which the Youth Hostels Association (England and Wales) can reach this market segment on a limited budget.

Figure 3.1 Short Holidays. Where do they stay?

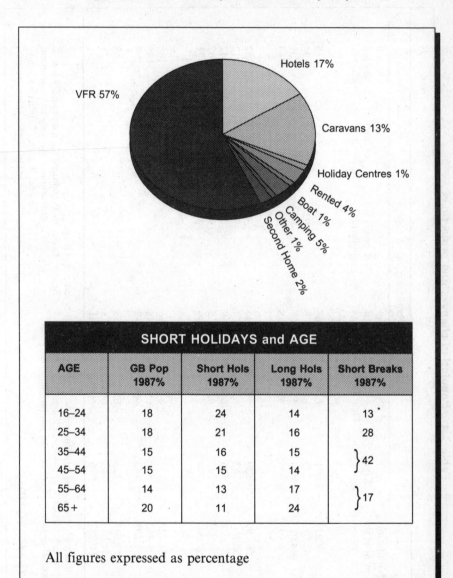

SHORT HOLIDAYS and AGE				
AGE	GB Pop 1987%	Short Hols 1987%	Long Hols 1987%	Short Breaks 1987%
16–24	18	24	14	13 ˙
25–34	18	21	16	28
35–44	15	16	15	}42
45–54	15	15	14	
55–64	14	13	17	}17
65 +	20	11	24	

All figures expressed as percentage

Source: English Tourist Board, *Insights* (1990).

Table 3.4 Population changes and projections

United Kingdom	Population at start of period	Average annual change					Thousands
		Live births	Deaths	Net natural change	Net civilian migration	Other adjustments[1]	Overall annual change
Census enumerated							
1901-1911	38,237	1,091	624	467	-82		385
1911-1921	42,082	975	689	286	-92		194
1921-1931	44,027	824	555	268	-67		201
1931-1951	46,038	785	598	188	25		213
Mid-year estimates							
1951-1961	50,290	839	593	246	-9	15	252
1961-1971	52,807	963	639	324	-32	20	312
1971-1981	55,928	736	666	69	-44	17	42
1981-1988	56,352	745	657	88	10	4	102
1988-1989	57,065	778	639	139	38	-6	171
Projections[2]							
1991-1996	57,333	835	649	186		0	186
1996-2000	58,462	801	654	148		0	148
2001-2006	59,201	743	653	89		0	89
2006-2011	59,648	725	657	68		0	68
2011-2016	59,989	747	668	78		0	78
2016-2025	60,381	776	695	81		0	81

[1] Changes in numbers of armed forces plus adjustments to reconcile differences between estimated population change and the figures for natural change and net civilian migration.

[2] 1988-based projections.

Source: Office of Population Censuses and Surveys; Government Actuary's Department; General Register Office (Scotland); General Register Office (Northern Ireland)

Adapted from *Social Trends,* 21 (1991).

Table 3.5   Great escapes survey 1988

533 Respondents

Responses (%)
Male   57.6   Female   42.4
Single   85.7   Married   14.3

Under 16*	13.0
16–19	18.0
20–24	21.5
25–34	25.0
35–44	10.0
45–54	7.0
55–64	3.0
65+	1.5
Unstated	1.0

* The promotion is targeted at young people but there are no age barriers in the YHA

Employment   (%)
Full-time   57.0
Part-time   2.0
Self-employed   4.0
Student   32.0
Retired   3.0
None   2.0

Occupation   (%)
Management/Professional   33.5
Technician   6.0
Office work   15.0
Trade/Craft   3.2
Manual   5.3
Student   32.0
Retired   3.0
None   2.0

Were you a YHA member before your 'Great Escapes' Holiday?
　　　(%)　　　　　(%)
Yes   71.0   No   29.0

If so, have you been on a 'Great Escapes' Holiday Before?
	(%)		(%)	
Yes	28.0	No	72.0	[Base 378]

If so what sort of holiday?

	(%)
Multi-activity	21.0
Watersports	24.0
Rocksports	7.0
Airsports	8.0
Walking	20.0
Cycling	5.0
Skiing	1.0
Riding	8.0
Sand Yachting	1.0
Golf	1.0
Incomplete	4.0

[Base 106]

Where did you find out about 'Great Escapes'?

	(%)
YHA Magazine	44.0
Brochure	20.0
Friend	10.0
Member	2.5
YHA Shop	3.5
Hostel	1.0
National Office	2.0
YHA News	1.0
Other magazine	6.0
Handbook	2.5
Travel Agent	1.0
Other	3.0
No Answer	2.0

Other results showed that users were very satisfied with the product, some had transport difficulties to the locations, travelled on their own or in twos to the holiday, were particularly impressed by hostel and training staff.

Source: Youth Hostels Association (England and Wales), Commissioned Market Research.

References

1. P. Kotler, *Principles of Marketing* (Prentice-Hall, 1990).
2. P. M. Chisnall, *Marketing: A Behavioural Analysis* (McGraw Hill, 1985).
3. V. T. C. Middleton, *Marketing in Travel and Tourism* (Heinemann, 1988).
4. Kotler *Principles of Marketing*.

The author gratefully acknowledges the assistance of the Youth Hostels Association (England and Wales) in the preparation of this case study. Certain aspects have been amended to maintain confidentiality of data.

4 Mersey Ferries: Ferry 'Cross the Mersey

L&R LEISURE PLC

Objectives

(a) To understand the process of product modification
(b) To introduce the issue of product positioning in the market place
(c) To introduce the management of change

Transport or Tourism

One of the most difficult tasks for the marketeer is to reposition a product in the market place when it is approaching the end of its life cycle. There are, however, successful examples worthy of consideration. Steam railways of all sizes and descriptions have been relaunched during the past 30 to 40 years as visitor attractions, having been primarily a form of transport for the preceding 80 to 100 years: witness the thriving Bluebell and Severn Valley leisure railway lines. The older 'holiday camps' have been remodelled and repositioned as multi-activity holiday centres known as 'Holiday Worlds' or by other similar names. Former textile mills are now heritage centres and working museums attracting large numbers of visitors.

This case study is about the repositioning of the Mersey Ferries, but there is a difference. While being primarily marketed as a leisure facility the ferries still have to provide a transport service meeting the requirements of a residual journey-to-work demand from Merseyside passengers.

The Product Concept

Kotler[1] defines a product as:

> anything that can be offered to a market for attention, acquisition, use or consumption that might satisfy a want or need. It includes physical objects, services, persons, places, organisations and ideas.

He then continues to develop the product concept as a three-level entity:

- **Core product**, which is the real reason for the purchase, the main benefit sought – such as a cheese and salad sandwich satisfying a hunger pain in the stomach
- **Tangible product**, which is the main characteristic on offer, such as the features, quality, brand and packaging of the core product – in the case of the sandwich, the type of cheese, the freshness, the wrapping
- **Augmented product**, which is an additional service and benefit, such as customer service, information, guarantees and warranty – in our example, this would include the way in which the sandwich is sold (with or without a smile), the guarantee 'sell by date' on the wrapping, etc.

Some practitioners would include elements of the Tangible and indeed Augmented product as essential to the Core product in terms of tourism provision. The importance of customer service is a point in question. Is it part of the Core product or not?[2]

The Product Life Cycle

The case study also involves a consideration of the product life cycle concept and its possible application in such a situation. The basic concept of the life cycle attempts to explain the stages through which a product usually passes. In this way, companies can plan for the modification or deletion of products in the latter stages of their life cycle. They can also plan for the introduction of new products. Figure 4.1 illustrates the product life cycle model, and the five stages from development to decline are summarised below:

1. **Development** – Creation of awareness, trial in the market place
2. **Growth** – Broadening of the market, far faster uptake of product, marketing expenditure of development stage comes to fruition; opportunity for profit
3. **Maturity** – Competitors enter the market place, sales growth slackens and so do profits
4. **Saturation** – Peak reached and changing behaviour patterns emerge in a competitive market
5. **Decline** – Sales and profits move into a continuous decline as new or modified products are developed and buyers switch allegiance.

This generalised approach is still favoured by marketeers because it has a simple appeal and many products actually exhibit this pattern of performance. Nevertheless, critics argue that there are so many exceptions to the generalised concept that its usefulness is overstated. Timescales are also important. Some products sell well for decades with only minor modifications – bottled Guinness Extra Stout, for example. Others rise and fall within weeks, such as the one-off Christmas record or the sports-related fashion product. How do the Mersey Ferries fit the concept ? A useful discussion of the tourist product life cycle is presented by Cooper, in his chapter on 'Tourist Product Life Cycle'.[3]

Figure 4.1   The product life cycle: profit during the cycle

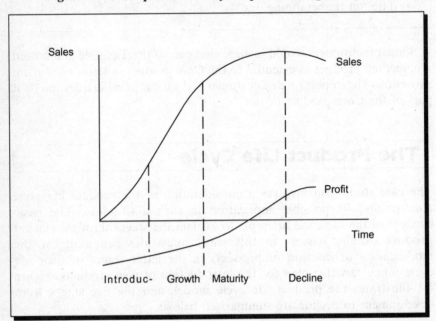

Product Positioning

The importance of image cannot be overstated in tourism marketing given the intangible nature of what is on offer. Moving from the image held by potential customers about short-distance public transport trips, whether it be by tube, bus, train or ferry, to a totally different image of a tourist attraction requires a considerable shift of emphasis. The image projection has to be based on a strong core product, an offering which will meet expectations and preferably have a unique or special selling point.

Restructuring an image is a crucial task for the marketeer, for if the product is not positioned appropriately within the market place visitors will not buy what is being offered – or if they do buy it and are disappointed their word of mouth marketing will be far too negative to encourage others.

Product positioning is thus the very practical task of specifying how a product should be developed or modified to meet customer expectations while at the same time projecting an appropriate image to the target group(s) while the product is in an embryonic stage. This is a strong feature of the Mersey Ferries case study.

The Case

Since the granting of a Royal Charter by Edward III in 1330 there has been a ferry of some description on the River Mersey ever since medieval times. It is thus not surprising that the Mersey Ferries are steeped in history and folklore. The modern ferry service, however, was first introduced as a steam boat crossing in the 1820s and peaked in the 1920s when thousands of people travelled to work by boat on weekdays and used the same facility to escape to the holiday resort of New Brighton and the Wirral at weekends and Bank Holidays.

With the provision of an improved rail and road structure linking Liverpool, Birkenhead and the Wirral the ferries since the 1930s suffered a steadily declining patronage, although in recent years this stabilised (see Table 4.1). In 1974, the operation of the ferry routes came under the responsibility of Merseyside Passenger Transport Executive, a local government-based transport coordinating body responsible for all public transport in the Merseyside metropolitan area. Its parent, the county authority was scrapped in the early 1980s, but a residual organisation, the Merseyside Passenger Transport Authority and Executive, with a trading name Merseytravel, inherited the responsibility for the heavily loss-making Mersey Ferries. In 1989/90 the cost of carrying approxi-

Figure 4.2   Mersey Ferries: routes before 1990

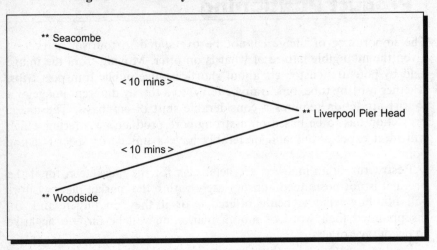

Operational Timetable: Boat leaving Pier Head for each destination every 15 mins.

mately one million passengers between Liverpool Pier Head and Wood-side and Seacombe (see Figure 4.2) was £2.5 million in subsidy.

In 1988, Merseytravel decided that the Mersey Ferries could no longer be sustained as a commuter facility and that even with reinvestment in the boats the traditional flow of journey-to-work traffic would never be regained. Initial market research survey work (see Figure 4.3) indicated that 50 per cent of weekday travel already used the services for leisure purposes and over 90 per cent at weekends. L&R Leisure plc, leisure and business strategy consultants (see Figure 4.4) was commissioned to present a feasibility study as to whether it would be possible to reposition Mersey Ferries as a leisure attraction rather than primarily a ferry crossing

Table 4.1   Mersey Ferries: single cross-river passenger trips

1983–84	1,541,000
1984–85	1,800,000
1985–86	1,668,000
1986–87	1,800,000
1987–88	1,803,000
1988–89	1,960,000

Source: Merseytravel statistics.

Figure 4.3   Market research activity

A Range Of Market Research Activities Has Been Undertaken

During the course of the project we have carried out a range of market research activities. These have included:

* a review of regional and Merseyside leisure and tourism statistics, from tourist board statistics and other available survey data.

* a CACI/ACORN survey on the resident population within 0-60 minutes, 60-90 minutes and 90-120 minutes of Pier Head. This socio-demographic data is available as a separately bound technical document.

* a set of surveys, by interviewer questionnaire, carried out during May 1989, on various populations relating to the Mersey Ferries.
  These comprise:

  Ferry Passengers, weekdays

  Weekend and bank holidays

  Visitors at Liverpool attractions

  Royal Iris cruise passengers

  The survey data is available as separately bound technical documents.

* a series of Focus Group sessions, with structured discussions on Ferry related issues, conducted with small groups of people representing Merseyside tourist interests.

* a telephone questionnaire with a representative sample of 1988 educational cruise teachers/leaders.

* a review of the current market for charter and corporate hire.

  The customer profile is summarised below:

Who Are Ferry Passengers?

Weekdays

- 61% are from the C2DE socio-economic group with 39% from ABC1

- the bulk (50%) are leisure travellers. 40% are business travellers
a- 81% were Merseysiders

- the single biggest source of Ferry passengers was Wirral (43%); next was Liverpool with 30%

- 82% of those from outside Merseyside are leisure passengers

- nearly two-thirds of passengers from Liverpool were leisure, whilst for Wirral it was one-third

- 48% were travelling alone; 20% were families (16% with children); 18% were couples and 15% were with friends. There were no organised groups.

Continued over

Weekends

- *Biggest category was families with children (40%). 25% were travelling alone, 18% were couples, 12% were with friends and 4% were families without children. Only 1% were in an organised group (of 2 or more people).*

- *59% are from the C2DE socio-economic group with 41% from ABC1*

- *80% were Merseysiders*

- *the two biggest sources of Ferry passengers were Liverpool and Wirral with roughly a third each.*

BANK HOLIDAYS

- 65% ARE FROM THE C2DE SOCIO-ECONOMIC GROUP WITH 35% FROM ABC1

- NEARLY ALL WERE LEISURE TRAVELLERS. ONLY 6% WERE BUSINESS TRAVELLERS

- 76% WERE MERSEYSIDERS

- THE SINGLE BIGGEST SOURCE OF FERRY PASSENGERS WAS LIVERPOOL (35%) NEXT WAS WIRRAL WITH 27%

- 48% WERE FAMILIES (42% WITH CHILDREN); 24% WERE COUPLES; 18% WERE TRAVELLING ALONE; AND 10% WERE WITH FRIENDS. THERE WERE NO ORGANISED GROUPS.

Source: L&R Leisure PLC Business Plan.

Table 4.2   Basic service level

Time	Predicted Arrival Rate At Pier Head %	Number Arriving At Pier Head
10–11.00	9	104
11–12.00	14	164
12–13.00	17	200
13–14.00	16	187
14–15.00	22	258
15–16.00	16	187
16–17.00	6	70
Total	**100**	**1170**

table continued over

Month	%	Visitor Year 1	Visitor Year 3
January	1.5	3,750	6,000
February	2.5	6,250	10,000
March	7.0	17,500	28,000
April	9.0	22,500	36.000
May	10.0	25,000	40,000
June	12.0	30,000	48,000
July	15.0	37,500	60,000
August	19.0	47,500	76,000
September	13.0	32,500	52,000
October	7.0	17,500	28,000
November	2.5	6.250	10,000
December	1.5	3,750	6,000
Total	**100.0**	**250,000**	**400,000**

Source: L & R Leisure plc.

Furthermore, they were asked to assess market potential, the findings of which looked promising (see Figure 4.5).

L&R Leisure plc were asked to prepare a business and marketing plan to reposition the Mersey Ferries as a leisure-based operation, but with a task of maintaining some provision for the residual commuter market.

It is also important to note that Merseyside during the 1980s developed a series of visitor attractions, particularly through the re-use of redundant buildings and derelict land. Britain's first National Garden Festival (1984) was a prime example, attracting approximately 3.5 million visitors. The reinvestment in the Grade I listed buildings at Albert Dock, which now houses Europe's biggest Maritime Museum and the new Tate Gallery Liverpool as well as many commercial outlets, signified a further commitment to redevelopment for leisure purposes. It is estimated that Albert Dock is Britain's second most popular free tourist attraction, with over 4 million visitors per annum.

Much of the impetus for this redevelopment has been generated by the Merseyside Development Corporation which has a committed approach to upgrading the riverside through re-use of one-time maritime facilities. The tourist economy, however, is not based solely on the river. The world-famous pop group of the 1960s, the Beatles, grew up and started their careers in Liverpool and this is reflected in tour trails throughout the city together with 'The Beatle Story' and other attractions at Albert Dock. There is also a strong cultural and entertainment base which the

Figure 4.4   The L&R Leisure plc consultancy

20 YEARS IN LEISURE

As a consultancy, we have nearly twenty years' experience in the leisure industry; unlike most others, we also have current, hands-on experience. Our 'Royal Scotsman' luxury hotel train won a Queen's Award for Export in 1988, in recognition of an outstanding standard of service.

SEND INFORMATION
STAFF ON A CUSTOMER
CARE COURSE WITH NO
PRIOR BRIEFING

We have helped many, very different clients with their Quality Service performance, from large corporate groups to family firms, from trusts to seasonal attractions, including:

IDENTIFY
NEED FOR
TRAINING

Anglesey Sea Zoo
Cornish Association of Tourist Attractions
Hotel and Catering Training Board
Institute of Leisure and Amenity Management
Ironbridge Gorge Museum Trust
London Borough of Tower Hamlets
Manpower Services Commission

ATTEND COURSE
YOURSELF AND HEAR
STAFF AIR THEIR IDEAS
AND FRUSTRATIONS

RAF Museum Hendon
Rhondda Heritage Park
Science Museum
Sports Council
Wembley Stadium Limited

By spending time with you, your team and your customers, and then developing a programme for your specific needs, L & R could help you, too, to make the breakthrough to a more productive Quality Service Cycle.

COMPLETE
THOROUGH TRAINING
PROGRAMME.
ADVANCE 2 SPACES

EVERONE SEES CHAIRMAN
LEAVE CUSTOMER CARE
SESSION EARLY FOR A
LUNCH APPOINTMENT.
BACK 2 SPACES.

THINK 'THANK HEAVEN
THAT'S OVER, WE CAN
GET BACK TO NORMAL'.
BACK 4 SPACES

Source: L&R Leisure plc

Merseyside Tourist Board promoted under the banner 'Merseyside 90 . . . More than you ever imagined'.

L&R Leisure plc set out to establish just how the Mersey Ferries could be modified to match a market need for leisure travel, and yet accommodate a remit to provide a commuter service at peak times.

Figure 4.5 Market appraisal summary

In analysing the markets potentially available to the Mersey Ferries four distinct segments were identified:

(1) **Tourist and leisure market**
Day visitors from a home base up to two hours' drive time catchment (estimated 11.5 million people), 0–60 minutes' drive time 4.04 million people. These include the important sub-segments:
(a) Local residents – The population of Merseyside is 1,455,000
(b) Visiting Friends and Relatives – a third of Merseyside's 1.8 million staying visitors (600,000) are VFR and an estimated further 700,000 come to see relatives for a day visit, giving a total of £1.3 million.
(c) Tourists based in Merseyside commercial accommodation.
(d) Day visitors from near North West areas such as Chester or the Fylde coast resorts. In 1987 the North West attracted 11m UK and 900,000 overseas visitors.

(2) **Educational market**
Within Merseyside there are 795 schools. According to a CACI/ Acorn breakdown the number of children of school age within one hour is 650,000, within 1 hours 1.25 million, within 2 hours 1.8 million.

(3) Private Charter Market – In 1988 there were 111 private charter (non-educational) cruises, mainly social clubs. Corporate hospitality showed little demand beyond the North West.

(4) Cross-river Passenger Transport market.

Source: L&R Leisure plc

New business objectives, covering a 2–5-year time span, were drawn up:

- Operate the Mersey Ferries under a new image and as a separate business unit (i.e., as opposed to the mainstream activity of Merseytravel in coordinating local bus and train services)
- Develop some positive indicators of regeneration through this business and assist in raising the image of Merseyside
- Show a trend of improving 'profitability' against an annual subsidy from Merseytravel

- Develop and operate some shoreside leisure use – for example, new related visitor attractions
- Maintain a cross-river passenger service matched to market need

Within these overall objectives a series of shorter-term actions were outlined by L&R Leisure plc as the basis for Business Plan preparation:

(a) Prepare a realistic Business Plan, embracing capital cost requirements and how these could be funded; operational costs and revenue; marketing and promotional requirements; management and staffing proposals

(b) Set up a separate new business unit based on leisure operations and prepare it for the launching of a new service in April 1990

(c) Promote the concept of a leisure-based operation to staff; train and get their enthusiasm and support; prepare them for work in the new leisure-based operation

(d) Produce a shoreside development plan in conjunction with other partners such as Merseyside Development Corporation, Liverpool City Council, Wirral Borough Council, etc.

(e) Seek priming funds from Europe and other public sources

The Task

As a recent junior consultant engaged by L&R Leisure plc, you have been asked to work on the Mersey Ferries project, and draft sections of a preliminary discussion paper titled 'Developing the Core Product'. A colleague has prepared estimates of visitor use based on the market research exercises (see Table 4.2). You have been requested to work the findings into a saleable product.

1. What should be the Mersey Ferries' core product on offer to the public (this should include suggestions for improvements to the vessels and a proposed sailing timetable)?
2. What management and staff training should occur to ensure that staff form an integral part of this core product?
3. What facilities would you envisage for shore termini?

References

1. P. Kotler, *Principles of Marketing* (Prentice-Hall, 1990).
2. V.T.C. Middleton, *Marketing in Travel and Tourism* (Heinemann, 1988).
3. C. Cooper 'Tourist Product Life Cycle' in S.F. Witt and L. Moutinho, *Tourism Marketing and Management Handbook* (Prentice-Hall, 1989).

The author gratefully acknowledges the assistance of L&R Leisure plc and Merseytravel in the preparation of this case. Certain aspects have been amended to maintain confidentiality of data.

5 Marches Cycles: A Bicycle Company Made for Two

Objectives

(a) To introduce feasibility studies
(b) To understand the problems facing small businesses starting in tourism
(c) To introduce pricing strategies

Pricing

Pricing is in many respects the most difficult element of the marketing mix to determine with any degree of accuracy, despite the use of computerised spreadsheet packages to predict outcomes. It is difficult because price signals so much to the consumer. It is also hard to assess competitor reaction. In the tourism sector the price-quality dimension has been of increasing relevance as visitors have become more sophisticated in outlook. The grading and selection of overseas packages, including long-haul, for example, is almost a passion among the 'grey panther' segment with considerable disposable income.

Consumer preference is based on a concept which can be simply described as 'value for money'. The concept is complicated, however, in that different market segments attach different values to what they perceive as 'value'. An overseas visitor wishing to visit a stately home which he or she had read about in an enlightening guide book might find a £5 entrance fee perfectly acceptable, but a visitor from 50 miles away could well question the value of such an admission price.

Cost

One confusion that often arises, even in terms of the terminology used, is the difference between 'cost' and 'price'. The former means the sum of all direct expenses incurred in providing a tourism service, and the latter is what an organisation decides it should sell its service for. Accurate costing is vital, and in the long run pricing should more than cover the cost of a particular service (whereas in some instances, in the short term, a company might price below cost).

The total cost of providing a service is usually divided into two component parts, fixed and variable costs. For example, the fixed costs in running a hotel are very high. The building, and the fixtures and fittings, account for the major share of cost in providing an accommodation service with a rate of return expected over a decade rather than a year or two. These costs are incurred regardless of the numbers of guests using the hotel. The variable cost, however, refers to the additional cost of providing services to fluctuating numbers of customers. For example, the cost of food and refreshment is variable in that the cost of provision varies according to how many guests have to be fed. The same applies to many visitor attractions such as steam railways or theme parks which have very high fixed costs in comparison to variable costs.

Price Elasticity of Demand

Pricing, on the other hand, is one of the key signals to the customer about the nature of the service on offer. In this respect, the individual makes a judgement as to whether the price is in an acceptable range. The relationship between the quantity bought (which is a dependent variable) and the change in price (an independent variable) which causes it is referred to as the 'price elasticity of demand'. Where there is considerable competition in the market place (i.e. it is easy for a customer to switch from one supplier to another or choose readily between very similar offerings), pricing is sensitive. In such circumstances, a price reduction will lead to a noticeable switch in favour of that particular offering. Generally speaking, if revenue accruing from such price reductions exceeds revenue loss from such a reduction, the service is classified as 'price elastic'. For example, coach companies running day excursions or mini-breaks to resorts such as Blackpool find demand very price elastic. If prices are low, demand is sustained; if prices are high, demand drops as the consumer seeks a bargain elsewhere. In many respects, the quality of the coach and driver is secondary to a cheap price.

In comparison, where price is a less acute factor in the purchasing decision, price elasticity is said to be inelastic (i.e. the proportionate change in demand in contrast to price is less significant). Thus, if price is increased by 20 per cent and yet demand recedes by only 2 per cent the service is described as inelastic. Travel on the Orient Express, first-class business travel by rail to London over medium distances, the hiring of distinctive country cottages during the summer school holiday all fit into this categorisation.

One of the major problems confronting small companies in the tourism sector, especially when establishing a business, is how to develop a suitable pricing strategy which meets projected demand for their service. However, once location and positioning in the market place have been resolved it becomes clearer how a company can price to meet its objectives. For example, a company seeking to become market leader might well price lower than main competitors in order to secure volume. Equally so, an organisation offering a very differentiated service and seeking a niche market would tend to adopt a premium pricing strategy.

So far, pricing has been discussed in a strategic sense. For example, many suppliers from tour operators to theme parks have adopted an 'all-inclusive' pricing policy. Other companies have applied strategies which feature lower initial pricing but with add-ons afterwards. For example, hotel groups involved in joint promotions offer accommodation at peppercorn sums but with the stipulation that certain meals have to be bought during the weekend break. Calculated within this approach is a reckoning that the guest will also spend so much on other in-house facilities, such as the bar.

At the same time, price is used as a tactical marketing tool. It is applied as a short-term marketing method to shift patterns of demand. Tactical selling of package holidays through discounting, hotels offering substantial cuts in rack rates for groups in order to improve Sunday night occupancy levels, holiday centres offering value-added packages to groups when demand is low at the beginning or end of the main season are examples of tactical price cutting. Pricing in these circumstances, often married to a short burst of promotional activity, can very often be justified on a marginal costing basis (i.e., the price reflects variable costs and a smaller than usual contribution to fixed overheads).

The Case

Two young entrepreneurs returning home to the border country of England and Wales decided that with a heightened awareness of Green issues there would be an increasing role for small-scale environmentally sensitive businesses within the tourism sector. Both had retained an interest in cycling since their childhood days and decided to establish a cycle hire and holiday company called Marches Cycles.

The question of location had been the first issue to resolve. They certainly wished to establish their business within the Marches, the brand name for the England-Wales borderland recently promoted by a consortium including the Heart of England Tourist Board and the Wales Tourist Board. The extract from an early promotional brochure in Figure 5.1 admirably introduces the reader to the features of the area.

Figure 5.1   Promoting the Marches

A country where 'an ancient wind is ceaselessly remembering ancient things', where 'farmhouses smell of bacon and herbs and burning sycamore and ash': so wrote Edward Thomas of Wales.

'The country for easy livers, the quietest under the sun' was how A.E. Housman described the border lands of England. The atmosphere of both countries is combined in the Marches, yet it has a special feel of its own, to do with the quality of landscapes and the rich quality of rural life in the small, unspoilt towns and villages, hamlets and farmsteads. Here wild and gentle Britain lie together: the high ridges of the Black Mountains give way to the orchards and hop yards and high flowering hedges of Herefordshire; the deep gorge of the Wye cuts into the Forest of Dean; and the weirdly named hills of Shropshire give way to the outwash plains of the Severn and Dee.

The partners were aware of successful cycle hire schemes established in Worcester, Hereford and Mid-Wales so were less inclined to choose these areas. However, Shropshire emerged as a county where the idea would fit beautifully, with so many quiet country lanes, delightful villages with old-fashioned shops, post offices and country inns. There seemed to be little or no competition providing cycle hire in South Shropshire.

Furthermore, there seemed to be a market within a two-hour travel band from Shrewsbury, Telford and the western zones of the West Midlands conurbation. They had calculated that a potential market of several million would be within an acceptable drive time of such a facility making cycle hire quite feasible for a good day out. The idea of attracting rail-borne customers, including those from overseas on InterRail and Brit Rail passes, appealed very much. With the introduction of 'Sprinter Trains' on the Marches rail line from Crewe to Cardiff, the carriage of passengers' bicycles had been restricted. British Rail, however, was known to be in favour of informing passengers of cycle hire schemes near to their stations. Marches Cycles thus felt that they could well introduce a joint marketing effort with British Rail which could be incorporated into the full-colour line guide promoting the route.

Marches Cycles therefore felt that a site at or near to one of the railway stations on the line would be ideal. It might even be possible to use an existing railway building if space was available, or secure a piece of land in one of the old goods yards or sidings long since redundant for rail purposes. Given this, the company began to seek sites in Church Stretton, Craven Arms, Ludlow or Leominster, the former three being in Shropshire, the latter in Hereford and Worcester. They appreciated that the purchase or leasing of premises and bicycles would constitute the bulk of fixed costs, a factor which was weighing heavy on their minds.

Their salaries would also have to be regarded as a fixed cost, but the partners were willing to accept very low returns during the first few years in order to make the company a success in the long run. They had secured financial support from relatives and one of the major banks on the basis of an outline business plan. However, the bank manager had requested that they strengthen their approach to pricing and be more precise in their estimate of projected revenue.

The partnership had been explicit about what it would offer the customer:

- Easy to ride bicycles in first-class mechanical order.
- Warm welcome including a free cup of tea, coffee or fruit juice for all bookers while waiting for their bicycle or on returning from their trip; this would not only be an ice breaker but allow for customer feedback in a more natural way
- Free brief instruction classes for beginners for a small sum
- A 'reasonable hours' back-up service guarantee in case of emergencies
- Self-guided routes for half-day, full-day, three-day and five-day tours
- With regard to the latter, a package including accommodation, luggage conveyance, personal guide and entrance charges to local attractions would be included in an overall promotion during peak periods of demand
- Full insurance cover would be included in return for a deposit on each hire transaction
- Delivery and collection of bicycles to local hotels and guest houses within a ten-mile radius of the centre
- Personal guide for parties of over ten based on the package mentioned above

---

Marches Cycles had spent months talking, albeit on a informal basis, to small hotels in the area who might be able to accommodate parties, make their guests welcome, offer good wholesome food and have a storage area for bicycles. Very few met all criteria, the major problem being capacity, but there seemed to be sufficient numbers to make a package feasible. Furthermore, a few were willing to discuss how standards could be improved to build up such business. Several hoteliers, however, felt that they could fill their rooms far easier with casual trade. This led to an investigation of farmhouse accommodation situated within close proximity who could look after small parties of cyclists in a more welcoming manner after a day's cycling. This part of the package could well be tested through the launch of two-night breaks as soon as Marches Cycles could handle it.

The range of bicycles would be to meet both the individual and family markets. There would be standard 3-and-5-speed bicycles, 10 speed cycles, tandems and children's bicycles on offer. There would also possibly be a range of 'Mountain Bikes', but itineraries had not been worked out for these as yet. It would depend on which location for the cycle hire business.

At the same time, Marches Tours had been recommended by a friend at Sheffield Polytechnic to seek the advice of a specialist consultancy, Transport For Leisure, based in Ilkley, Yorkshire. This company had for the past six years worked on a wide range of schemes involving transport and tourism from the development of long-distance walking holiday packages to feasibility studies of transport delights such as funicular railways. Marches Cycles were particularly uneasy about how to develop a pricing strategy which would reflect their overall product offering and their commitment to quality, while at the same time not being seen to be out of line with competitors in the field.

They therefore commissioned Transport For Leisure to produce a briefing paper on alternative pricing approaches which could sensibly be adopted by Marches Cycles. As a background document, Transport For Leisure has already been able to compare prices offered by a number of cycle hire companies and this is set out in Table 5.1 and 5.2.

The Task

As an associate of the consultancy, you have to prepare a briefing document advising on possible Pricing Strategies. The paper should also include a check list of matters which could form the basis of a short feasibility study.

Table 5. 1   A comparative survey of cycle companies – prices

Adults half-day hire	Price range £	Average price £	Number of companies
Standard/3-Speed	2.00–2.50	2.25	2
Child (Under 16)	1.50–3.00	2.16	3
Day or 24 hours			
3-Speed	3.50–5.00	4.14	4
5-Speed	3.50–5.50	4.50	2
10-Speed	6.00–9.00	7.60	3
Tandem (18-Gears)	14.00–20.00	17.00	3
All Terrain Bike			
10–18 Gears	6.00–10.00	8.66	3
21 Gears	10.00–16.00	12.80	3
2-Day Rate (Any Two Days or Weekend)			
3-Speed	7.00–9.50	8.16	3
5-Speed	5.00–11.00	8.00	2
10-Speed	10.00–18.00	14.66	3
All Terrain Bike			
10–18 Gears	8.00–20.00	15.33	3
21 Gears	13.00–32.00	22.33	3
Week			
3-Speed	17.50–28.00	23.44	4
5-Speed	17.50–27.50	22.50	2
10-Speed	30.00–45.00	38.33	3
All Terrain Bike			
10–18 Gears	28.00–50.00	42.66	3
21 Gears	45.50–90.00	65.17	3

Notes:

Methodology: Current brochures (1990) of the following organisations have been evaluated – Cadence Cycle Hire (Worcester), Joyrides (Machynlleth), Macclesfield and Vale Royal Groundwork Trust (Cheshire), Peak Cycle Hire (Peak National Park), Pedal Away (Herefordshire), Red Dragon Cycle Services (Borth).

No organisation offers identical service. Bicycle makes are different but fit generally into the categorisation shown above. All organisations offer basic advice, bicycle adjustment, bicycle repair kits and route planning. Some include insurance cover.

Weekly packages, including accommodation, etc. are so individualistic as to make comparison not worthwhile. Bicycle Beano (Herefordshire), for example, offer weekly guided tours with wholefood vegetarian cuisine in West Wales and the Marches either camping or indoor accommodation for between £170–£215. Joyrides offer Farmhouse, Easy Rider or Youth Hostel self-guided packages in Wales at a range between £175 and £245 but the package varies from accommodation only to Bed and Breakfast and Evening Meal.

Source: Transport For Leisure.

Table 5.2   Projected hirings and revenue

	Day hirings[*]	Estimated revenue (£)[**]
January	290	1430
February	280	1820
March	680	4420
April	956	6214
May	3050	19825
June	2090	13585
July	3045	19792
August	4025	26162
September	1890	12285
October	1200	7800
November	384	2496
December	272	1768
Totals	18162	117,597

[*] Day hirings refer to all bicycle hirings divided by days of operation
[**] Estimated revenue is calculated on a basis of average revenue per bicycle per day of £6.50

The figures are hypothetical, based on observations of several other bicycle hire centres, but must be treated as crude estimates

Source: Transport For Leisure.

References

J.C. Holloway and R.V. Plant, *Marketing for Tourism* (Pitman, 1988).

P. Kotler, *Marketing Management: Analysis Planning, Implementation and Control* (Prentice-Hall, 1988).

6   Air Miles: The World's Favourite Promotion

Objectives

(a) To understand the communications mix
(b) To introduce sales promotion as a strategic promotional tool
(c) To evaluate the nature of short-term action plans

Introduction: Promoting the Product

Most organisations attempt to develop an appropriate communications mix to transmit one (or a number of) important message(s) to potential or existing customers externally, and also to staff internally. For example, when a new product or service is launched, the main objective is to achieve high awareness levels amongst the target audience in the shortest time span possible. Within this overall communications or promotional mix there are a variety of tools, such as advertising, public relations, personal selling and direct marketing and sales promotion.

Sales Promotion

Sales promotion may be defined as a set of techniques used by marketeers to stimulate the potential buyer into making a purchase by way of an incentive over and above the usual product/service offering. The aim is to present customers with an opportunity to add value to their transaction by receiving some form of special offer, gift, collectable voucher, etc. as well as the core benefit offered. Sales promotions are not geared to customers only, but also to sales representatives, distributors and retailers so that they push goods through the distribution system as well as creating demand pull from the customer.

Sale promotion is particularly well developed in the fast-moving consumer goods market where short-term tactical campaigns are launched to boost sales of a given product on the supermarket shelves. The collection of on-pack vouchers, inserted cards, packets of seeds, small toys and sachets of hair shampoo are very commonplace. Such promotions tend to have a limited timescale, and form part of a wider promotional campaign which includes special packaging, innovative merchandising and an advertising campaign. As sales promotion techniques have been associated mainly with short-term campaigns most definitions reflect this. This case study, however, introduces sales promotion as a longer-term strategic sales approach to the market.

Such 'below the line' techniques (in contrast to 'above the line' advertising) have not been used so extensively in tourism promotions. Most of the major campaigns in recent years have been transport-related such as the joint Persil-British Rail free ticket offer which proved to be very successful in generating off-peak business. Hotel groups have engaged in similar joint ventures offering weekend breaks at specially discounted rates to buyers of bread, cereals and other household food items. Sales promotion techniques have been used by attractions which have joined forces with daily newspapers or companies such as Rowntree in the 'Kit Kat' leisure promotion of the mid-1980s offering a variety of recreationally-based incentives including discounted access to attractions throughout the UK to those who purchased a required number of Kit Kat confectionery bars.

Several company-based incentive travel schemes have also been developed, rewarding employees mainly by offering packaged hotel breaks as an incentive for meeting sales targets, but this type of sales promotion has not been on a significant scale in Britain.

The key motivational factor behind such schemes has been a desire on behalf of the manufacturer of a product to enhance their offering in the short term by providing a leisure-related incentive to the customer. The tourism sector has benefited by generating marginal business at times of spare capacity, such as bednights at weekends out of the main season. There are, of course, other objectives such as extending brand exposure, heading off competition, increasing market share, or exploring the business-to-business market in a measured way. The major forms of sales promotion which have been applied in tourism are listed in Table 6.1.

Table 6.1 Sales promotions

Technique	Target	Example
Price reduction	Direct to customer	Early bookers of package holidays receive cash
Competitions	Direct to customer/ Intermediary staff incentive	Very commonplace in newspapers, magazines Free holiday for winners
Vouchers/Coupons	Direct to customer	Collect an allotted number within a time limit and customer receives a discount, two for the price of one, etc.
More product	Direct to customer	Time related offer – buy now and customer can stay an extra night for the price of a weekend break
Free gifts	Direct to customer/ Intermediary staff	Timeshare sales are renowned for this technique
Clubs	Direct to customer	Additional benefits to regular customers to encourage them to buy more
Collector schemes	Direct to customer	Visit so many attractions, hotels etc. to have a 'passport' stamped
Prize draws	Direct to customer	Many localised schemes
Cash/Travel prizes	Intermediary staff	Based on sales of packages, etc.
Travel incentives	Business to business/ Company promotions	Incentive business – weekends, holidays for good performers

Tactical Plan

The tactical plan, a term sometimes used to refer to a short-span programme of action and on other occasions as a response to a fast-moving market situation, is becoming more commonplace in tourism marketing. In this case study, Air Miles, the task is related to the preparation of a tactical plan to launch a major strategic sales promotion campaign. The message and medium for each partner (the customer, the promoter and British Airways) needs to be clarified, however, for such a plan to succeed. There is also a need for actions to be sequenced, prioritised and scheduled. The core of the tactical plan will in this instance form the basis on which to build a five-year marketing plan.

The Case

While the staff at Air Miles, a subsidiary company of British Airways plc had been planning ahead for the introduction of an exciting concept known as Air Miles for some time, it was in the early days of 1988 that the organisation felt that it was time to prepare for a launch of this novel concept. The aim of Air Miles was to bring three distinct groups together in the market place by way of a 'collector' sales promotion. How to achieve this, however, was a far more difficult task. Air Miles was not just to be another short-term tactical promotion, but rather a strategic long-term marketing tool which would have lasting benefits.

Market Research

As with any new product, a judicious amount of desk research was carried out during the idea generation stage, and a thorough evaluation of the concept. The results of the research activities formed the basis of a SWOT analysis (Strengths, Weaknesses, Opportunities, Threats) which may be summarised as in Figure 6.1.

Figure 6.1   SWOT analysis of the market

1.   Sales promotion in the UK
In 1988 it was estimated that £15 billion was being spent on advertising and promotion in the UK. Of this, over £8 billion was devoted to non-media activities such as public relations, competitions, and sponsorship. Despite this, the market was not seen as being mature by any means, particularly as the numbers of very large multi-branded promotions were exceedingly limited. In fact, sales promotions were being used mainly as a tactical tool rather than a longer-term strategic marketing method of generating sales.

Air Miles also observed that there was no direct competitor in the field although there were a considerable number of single-brand loyalty promotions in several markets such as finance or motor vehicles. Thus, there was obviously an opportunity to be explored.

2. Overseas travel market

A brief overview of the market showed that:

- 28 million overseas holidays were taken in 1988, and that the growth had been consistent over the past 14 years.
- The number of holidays taken overseas had doubled since 1975, from 14 per cent in 1975 to 30 per cent in 1987/8.
- Expenditure by UK residents going abroad was £8,127 million in 1988.
- 68 per cent of UK adults had holidayed abroad, but never more than 30 per cent in one particular year.
- The only age segment that did not holiday overseas significantly was the 65 plus segment. All other age segments varied between 30 and 37 per cent travelling overseas in any one year.
- Holiday taking by social class showed that the AB and C1 groups accounted for 31 per cent of the population but took 58 per cent of overseas holidays while socio economic groupings C2, D abd E made 60 per cent of the population and accounted for only 41 per cent of overseas holidays.

3. The travel business

British Airways have clearly become market leader in the UK scheduled airline market but in contrast the European and long-haul markets were considered to be highly fragmented with well over 100 suppliers offering scheduled seats from UK airports.

The UK travel market was dominated by four big brand names – Thomson Travel Group, Intasun, Horizon and Redwing. Intasun collapsed soon afterwards. The travel trade distribution market, however, was more fragmented, but with six large chains dominating the market – Lunn Poly, Thomas Cook, Pickfords, Hogg Robinson, Co-op Travel and W.H. Smiths.

4. Wider economic and social trends

Other relevant trends were researched:

- **Commoditisation**: In many markets, it had become increasingly difficult for producers and retailers to differentiate their offerings to customers.
- **Widening horizons**: Holidays were being seen more as a necessity than a luxury, and customers were becoming more discerning and at the same time more adventurous in their pursuit of destinations.
- **Economy**: At the time, the economy was relatively stable with an increasing disposable income to more affluent groups in society.
- **Technology**: Advances in computerised inventory control for airlines meant that estimates of unused capacity could be predicted far more accurately.

The conditions thus looked promising for the establishment of a major strategic sale promotion related to travel.

The Concept

At a briefing meeting of marketing staff the Marketing Director outlined the core concept of Air Miles, as in Figure 6.2.

Figure 6.2   The Air Miles concept

The Air Miles concept is in many respects unusual in that it is designed to add value for the three participating groups:

The Consumer
The incentive for the consumer is travel at no cost. After purchasing goods or services from a variety of companies participating in the Air Miles scheme, consumers receive Air Miles vouchers. They continue collecting until they have saved enough to fly to their chosen destination, cashed in for discounts on package holidays or for optional extras such as car hire or hotel accommodation.

COLLECTING PATTERN CASE STUDY	
Mr Jeffrey Turner	Air Miles
Registered January 1989	collected
Air Miles Bonus	50
National Westminster	
Visa Card	35
Shell Collect & Select	75
Automobile Association	100
Allied Carpets	250
Texas Homecare	50
Austin Rover	300
Daily Express	40
Total	900

In July 1989 Mr Turner booked two
return flights to Paris

However, as well as being targeted to a distinctly young and upwardly mobile segment of the consumer market, Air Miles can also be used as a sales promotion technique for company to company business, as a tactical device to stimulate distribution channels, or simply as a staff incentive.

The Promoter
For the promoter company wishing to participate in the promotional scheme, the key benefits can be summarised as follows:

● Offer perceived difference from competitors in the market place
Only one major company in each sector is allowed to participate in the scheme. Thus, in the highly competitive area of credit card marketing National Westminster has become the Air Miles partner.

● Build customer loyalty
Collecting Air Miles leads to repeat business, habitual purchasing and hence strong customer loyalty. Thus, in the petroleum market Shell has strategically developed an Air Miles promotion to generate repeat business.

● Increase the value of a sale
Not only is the customer perception one of added value over and above the normal transaction, Air Miles is seen as a way of encouraging purchasers to buy more or buy premium priced goods in order to qualify for additional Air Miles. In this way the average spend per customer is increased as well as encouraging new customers.

● Motivate staff
In a similar manner Air Miles can be used by companies as an incentive to staff. The more they sell, the more Air Miles they receive as a bonus.

● Generate leads
As a tactical campaign Air Miles can be used to seek new customers by generating leads or mailing lists.

● Launch a product
To heighten the impact of a new product Air Miles can be used as an incentive to encourage use of such a facility. In a more emphatic way, it can be used to create instant awareness.

Thus, to the promoter Air Miles is very flexible in that it can be both a strategic promotion or a short-term tactical initiative within an overall marketing plan. Furthermore, the degree of exclusivity adds considerable appeal.

The Airline – British Airways
The major benefit to this major international airline will be the sale of spare capacity at a marginal cost, seats that would otherwise go unfilled. This also generates a new customer base and increased brand loyalty. Therefore, British Airways can increase their overall net revenue without diluting traffic.

It is our task to plan ahead accordingly and make Air Miles happen.

The Task

Within this context, as a market executive in the Air Miles marketing team, you are given the responsibility for preparing a one-year tactical marketing plan with an overall aim to launch Air Miles successfully as a long-term, sophisticated quality marketing concept on a mass market scale. Budgetary considerations will be discussed later. You have to detail the major tactical areas first, and these will be refined with cost implications at a later stage.

The specific objectives of the plan are:

(1) By the launch data in ten months' time secure 20 key promoters and between 50–80 other promoters so that Air Miles will be on offer in at least 10,000 retail outlets during its first year of operation
(2) To attract two million households to collect Air Miles
(3) To position Air Miles in the consumer's mind as the most attractive up-market and exclusive promotion
(4) To gain acceptance within the travel trade that the concept generates incremental holiday travel, and thereby enhances their own business
(5) To launch Air Miles successfully in the subsidiary business-to-business and staff incentives markets, thereby generating 1000 serious requests within the first six months of the launch.

References

J.C. Holloway and R.V. Plant, *Marketing For Tourism* (Pitman, 1988) Chs 7, 9, 11, 12.
V.T.C. Middleton, *Marketing in Travel and Tourism*, (Heinemann, 1988) Part four.

The author gratefully acknowledges the assistance of Air Miles in the preparation of this case. Certain aspects have been amended to maintain confidentiality of data.

7 Great British City Breaks: Marketing Consortium

GREAT BRITISH
CITIES

Objectives

(a) To evaluate different channels of distribution for the sale of short break packages
(b) Assess ways of selling to groups

Channels of Distribution

Distribution in terms of tourism marketing embraces two distinct aspects: the physical location of destinations and the channels of communication between the supplier and the customer. Tourism destinations and accommodation providers are very dependent on effective channels to sell their offerings to potential customers. In this instance, the case study reflects on the methods currently used by the Great British City Breaks consortium in getting their product offering to the market.

The selection of appropriate channels is vital to the success of any tourism product, bearing in mind the maxim 'Consumption is a function of availability'.[1] Selection, however, tends to be made on a cost basis first, then on the degree of control in the process and lastly with regard to service levels. These factors are, in fact, usually very closely ranked.

The channels may be summarised as follows:

Direct
Direct (or short channels) between the supplier and the customer. An outdoor activity breaks centre, for example, might send its brochure to Tourist Information centres where the customer peruses it and telephones a booking through direct to the company concerned.

Tour operator or wholesaler
Use of an intermediary. Tour operators develop packages for sale and sell direct to customers by way of their brochures. They are in reality acting on behalf of a group of suppliers who make up the composite product.

    Sometimes a group of suppliers forms a consortium to market their products collectively as a wholesaler – for example, the seaside resorts involved in The Waves promotion or Country Village Weekend Breaks in the West Midlands.

Travel agencies
Travel agencies are the retailers of the tourism business sector selling packages developed by suppliers themselves or through tour operators. The line of distribution is thus much longer, involving a supplier, a wholesaler and a retailer.

The channels of distribution have to be strongly related if the service offering is to reach the market place with any degree of success. This involves good promotional material, staff guide books and training sessions, staff incentives such as competitions and bonuses for high sales levels, familiarisation trips, and above all a commitment among the companies concerned to the service product on offer.

The Case

Launched in September 1986 by the well-known Radio 4 Broadcaster, Brian Redhead, Great English City Breaks, now known as Great British City Breaks, appealed very much to the media and to the travel trade. Established by a consortium of thirteen large cities in England (see Tables 7.1 and 7.2) this unusual short-break package had been put together months ahead by a Cities Marketing Group comprising tourism officers from each respective destination. The overall aim of the Group, as expressed in the minutes of the inaugural meeting was:

To promote England's larger provincial cities as places to stay in, particularly for short break holidays, by way of co-ordinating marketing activities, thus increasing the business to cities not traditionally associated with tourism.

Thus, from the outset the wide ranging objectives were to:

> (a)   Achieve economic and social benefits to the Cities
> (b)   Gain national recognition and support for the Cities
> (c)   Develop an image of the Cities as tourist destinations

The main activity of the Cities Marketing Group from 1986 to 1989 concentrated on the creation and marketing of weekend breaks geared to the individual/family market. Two other major areas were

> (1)   The generation of group business, and
> (2)   Public relations work to generate higher awareness levels

From the outset, the Group decided to produce a 'stand-alone' brochure and sell weekend packages through the travel trade agents by way of a short-breaks package operator. During the first year, National Holidays became the tour operator responsible for generating individual customer bookings and Enterprise Travel handled group trade. A year later, however, Golden Rail (later to become Gold Star Holidays) superseded National Holidays as the tour operator. In the same period another city, Hull, joined the consortium.

Table 7.1   The Great British City Breaks

Destinations

> The Original Thirteen
>
> **Birmingham**
> The 'Big Heart' of England, a pulsating city surrounded by Olde Englande attractions – boasting a picturesque network of canals and a market place for all trades for the last 800 years! The birthplace of the Industrial Revolution.
>
> **Bradford**
> Birthplace and home of the famous children's TV character Sooty, an overwhelming choice of things to do for educational and special

interest groups. The finest industrial heritage, steam trains and canal trips. Abundant themes, sports and activities, from knitting and sewing to photography – walking or riding the moors. Top class shows at the Alhambra Theatre, and the only Imax cinema screen in Britain.

Coventry
A modern centre with a rich and varied history from Boadicea to the Birth of English Motoring. Contrast Cathedrals old and new and view Lady Godiva – the city's favourite heroine. On the doorstep of Warwickshire – the only city in Shakespeare Country.

Leeds
Yorkshire's vibrant centre and cultural metropolis – a city for variety from Opera North to Old Tyme Music hall, Harewood House to industrial heritage at Armley Mills and from Victorian shopping arcades to the Tropical World at Roundhay Park. Come and visit us soon.

Leicester
Founded by the Romans and with many medieval landmarks in close proximity within this compact city centre – heart of the shires and hunting country connected with the Battle of Bosworth and Naseby. Great for knitwear and hosiery with one of Europe's largest open air markets.

Liverpool
City Resort – home of soccer champions, birthplace of the Beatles and location of TV's Brookside. Gothic Anglican to strikingly modern Catholic Cathedrals. A great maritime past brought to life at Albert Dock on Liverpool's historic waterfront.

Manchester
One of the great Victorian cities of England: preserves the best of the old and new. Visit Coronation Street at Granada TV studios, enjoy exclusive shopping and unrivalled nightlife all within easy reach of the Peaks and Pennines.

Newcastle (No longer part of the consortium)

Nottingham
Legend, Lace and Literature combine in the 'Queen of The Midlands'. Fascinating museums and historic houses, splendid shops. One of England's great sporting cities too from horse racing to cricket. Follow the footsteps of Robin Hood and his Men!

Plymouth
Seaside city in the heart of the West Country with a rich seafaring heritage and fine natural harbour made famous by Drake, Hawkins and Raleigh. Outstanding views from the Hoe. International yacht racing and special events all year round.

Portsmouth
Take a break in the city that deserves its title 'Flagship of Maritime England' where historic ships, castles, forts and superb museums combine with all the attractions of a seaside resort. Take a trip to France, the Isle of Wight or explore the beautiful Hampshire countryside as part of your stay.

Southampton (No longer part of the consortium)

Stoke-on-Trent
Welcome to the capital of 'China' – visit world famous potteries like Wedgwood, hunt for bargains and experience Gladstone Working Pottery Museum. Explore and enjoy the thrills of Europe's premier leisure park at Alton Towers.

Addition in 1987

Hull
The Humber Bridge provides an elegant entrance to this historic mercantile city characterised by the Old Town with its narrow lanes, renovated warehouses and vibrant marina. Echoes of the sea and ships abound.

Additions in 1989

Dundee
Dundee, a city with 800 years of history and a modern outlook on life is surprisingly situated on several miles of River Tay waterfront. As a base for special interest groups or for touring the East of Scotland Dundee is in an ideal position.

Glasgow
Glasgow – A true Renaissance City. Steeped in culture, rich in history. Where you can sense the 'Buzz' as you walk through the streets lined with Europe's finest Victorian architecture. A city which provides year round entertainment to suit every taste. A city that has earned its title – Cultural Capital of Europe.

Cardiff
Cardiff, Capital City and gateway to Wales, is the current holder of Britain's City in Bloom award. It has an impressive Civic Centre in gleaming white Portland stone that is said to rival Washington.

Swansea
All year weather visitor centre. The ideal location for summer
holidays, off season breaks or exciting day trips. Ever popular
Swansea . . . gateway to some of the most magnificent scenery to be
found anywhere in Wales. Swansea also boasts excellent beaches
and a lively city centre.

Source: Great British City Breaks.

Marketing Campaign

The launch budget for the first year of the campaign amounted to
£130,000 from the Cities themselves. This was was matched by £120,000
from the English Tourist Board, thus providing an overall spend of
£250,000. This was spent mainly on the production and distribution of a
high quality full-colour brochure. 500,000 copies were distributed in 1986
and 800,000 printed in subsequent years to meet wider distribution
requirements. In the early days of the promotion an extensive public
relations campaign resulted in continual media coverage including prime
television time. Media coverage of the cities since 1986 has been
highlighted as a very successful outcome since the initial launch.

In September 1988, the consortium decided to extend its destination
coverage to include Scotland and Wales. The customer package was
subsequently renamed 'Great British City Breaks' and relaunched at the
World Travel Market in November 1988. Trade had grown (see Table
7.2) at a steady rate and in line with the significant growth in the short-
breaks market recorded elsewhere. Research had also indicated that
those taking City Breaks were predominatly of the AB socio economic
grouping (which was also verified by other main operators), being mainly
couples booking near to the date of travel.

Table 7.2   Great British City Breaks: Criteria for eligibility

Population over 175,000
A Tourism Marketing Officer
A sizeable tourism promotion budget
Membership of the Regional Tourist Board
Tourism not traditionally a major element of the city's economy

Source: Great British City Breaks.

The package

The essential ingredients of the City Breaks package have not altered considerably since the first year of operation. Potential customers have three ways in which to book a break. They pick up a brochure from their travel agent, post a coupon from a magazine advert/story, or telephone the tour operator direct to make a booking. The inclusive package on offer to the customer is as follows:

- Accommodation in a 3-or-4 star hotel with a full British breakfast for £21 per person per night (1989 Brochure price)
- An option of making one's own travel arrangements, referred to as a 'Freedom Break' or an inclusive package of hotel and standard-class rail travel from the customer's nearest home rail station to the chosen destination. First-class rail travel is offered on payment of a small supplement.
- Suggested itineraries and a limited amount of information about each destination is provided in the brochure.
- Availability – Friday, Saturday or Sunday nights for one to three nights' stay at any time of the year except for the Christmas period.
- Special discounts are available for children under 16 sharing a bedroom with two adults.
- A Weekend Car Hire deal is available in association with Europcar.

A package for groups had been devised on a similar basis with an opportunity to build in additional features such as visits to attractions and guided tours. The volume of business at 9769 bookings generated 24,167 bednights but the contract with Enterprise Travel was concluded. The potential of the groups market, however, was estimated to be far greater than that being realised at present.

Having spent three years launching and building up Great British City Breaks, the Cities Marketing Group decided that it would be appropriate to seek the advice of an impartial consultant to review progress and suggest strategies to be incorporated into a three-year rolling marketing plan.

The consultant's report was wide-ranging and generally reassuring about the way in which the Cities Marketing Group were building up the product on offer. There were, however, areas of concern which would require further discussion and action in the short term. Distribution of the brochures was one such area. The 'stand-alone' brochure was being despatched to travel agents in a satisfactory manner but research undertaken by the consultancy with several travel agents as well as the two main short-break tour operators – Superbreak and Rainbow – brought the following response:

- 75 per cent of travel agencies were aware of City Breaks, but only after prompting
- 33 per cent had used the brochure, but only very occasionally
- None had actively promoted it
- The majority indicated that far more business came from Superbreak and Rainbow breaks (with print runs of millions) and hence these were racked in preference to City Breaks
- There was a degree of confusion between City Breaks and the offerings of the above-mentioned operators; the issue of distribution thus required immediate attention

The Task

Following a discussion about the consultant's report it was agreed, amongst other matters, to table three items for urgent consideration at the next Cities Marketing Group strategy meeting:

(1) Group travel
(2) The main brochure and its distribution
(3) Direct Marketing

As a recently appointed marketing assistant to the Cities Marketing Group, you have to prepare summary papers on each of the three topics mentioned above. The group travel paper should be packed with ideas for enhancing group travel, and suggest possible ways of reaching the market both in the UK and in Europe. The paper on the brochure should marshall the arguments for and against the retention of the existing 'stand-alone' brochure, and present a recommendation. The direct marketing proposals should explore two ideas raised by the consultancy (1) A direct mail campaign, (2) Marketing to the residents of each participant city.

Tables 7.3, 7.4 and 7.5 show criteria for eligibility in the promotion, the 1988/89 expenditure budget, a a breakdown of origins and destinations in 1988/89.

Table 7.3   British City Breaks – campaign results 1986–9

Brochure dates	Passengers	Bednights	Nights per person
Sep 86–Sep 87	9378	29161	2.2
Sep 87–Mar 88	13466	19899	1.4
Apr 88–Mar 89	17951	30700	1.7
Mar 89–Mar 90	19100 *		
* Estimate Handled through 2000 Travel Agencies			

Source: Great British City Breaks

Table 7.4   1988/89 Expenditure budget

	£
Main brochure production	120000
Group Travel promotion	10000
Distribution/Merchandising	5000
Promotions:Sales Promotion	50000
Market Research	5000
Administration	7000
Total	197000

Source: Great British City Breaks

Table 7.5   Great British City Breaks – bookings analysis

City	Total passengers	% Split RI	FB
Birmingham	1792	49	51
Bradford	750	36	64
Coventry	546	36	64
Hull	333	34	66
Leeds	1557	42	58
Leicester	437	24	76

Liverpool	1953	54	46
Manchester	2576	50	50
Newcastle	2643	54	46
Nottingham	1011	40	60
Plymouth	1675	48	52
Portsmouth	996	46	54
Southhampton	1263	30	70
Stoke-on-Trent	617	25	75
Total	17951	46	54

Origin of bookings through travel agents (Winter 88/89)

	%
Scotland	21.9
North East	10.2
Yorkshire and Humberside	9.5
London	8.7
West Country	8.1
Wales	8.1
South East	8.0
East Anglia	6.2
Thames and Chilterns	5.3
North West	4.9
East Midlands	3.4
Cumbria	2.8
Heart of England	1.8
Southern	0.7
Channel Islands	0.4
	100.0

Rural	32.7
GBC City	14.5
London	8.8
Other cities	8.1
Other urban	35.9
	100.0

RI – Rail Inclusive Break
FB – Freedom Break (not rail inclusive)

Source: Great British City Breaks.

References

1. M.J. Baker, 'Maxims for Marketing in the Eighties', *Advertising* (Winter 1980).

You may also find the following of value:

A. Fitch Tour, 'Operators in the U.K.' *Travel and Tourism Analyst* (March 1987).

8 The English Riviera: Sun, Sea and Something Else

THE ENGLISH
RIVIERA
TORQUAY · PAIGNTON · BRIXHAM

Objectives

(a) To understand the concept of destination marketing
(b) To examine the relationship between product development and promotion in the context of a seaside resort

Destination Marketing

The concept of destination marketing is an exciting one – in particular the need to develop and modify new products, to satisfy both the changing aspirations of existing markets and to attract new custom are essential in an increasingly competitive environment. The task has become critical in the 1990s given that so many destinations could well be described as being in the 'decline' stage of their product life cycle, an issue very often discussed in relation to seaside resorts.[1] This case study highlights the importance of destination marketing and raises a number of issues, including product development, branding and theming.

Consumer Perception

The main concern of the case is, however, destination marketing. First, consider the meaning of the word 'destination'. In one sense, it is merely a dream in the potential holidaymaker's mind. As Seaton[2] comments:

A holiday is an invisible product that only materialises well after purchase. Unlike a car (which can be test-driven), a wine (which can be tasted), a coat (which can be seen and tried on) tourism has no verifiable presence that can be inspected before consumption. Tourism is pure anticipation – a bundle of expectations about satisfactions in another place at some specified future time

This concept has been referred to as 'intangibility' (i.e. the lack of physical evidence of any given tourism product until it is actually consumed). The purchase of a holiday involves the customer in the creation of a personal image about a resort and the potential benefits accruing from a visit or holiday. The image will not necessarily be based on a destination's functional aspects, such as good communications or a wide range of accommodation, but is attributable also to more general-ised perceptions such as friendliness of the host population, local attractions, walks along the promenade or 'happy times' or 'fun' at the seaside. Readers wishing to pursue this area of study will also find Telisman-Kosuta's[3] discussion of image and the marketing of destina-tions useful.

Branding

Inextricably linked with image projection is the concept of 'branding'. This powerful promotional tool aims, through the use of visual, symbolic and written means, to convey a distinctive and pleasing identity (in most instances) to the prospective customer. The concept has been well developed in terms of the marketing of fast-moving consumer goods. For example, in terms of supermarket merchandising, branding has to be very strong to differentiate similar products on the shelves. The same applies to High Street trading. Next and Burtons, Macdonalds and Burger King compete to attract the attention of the shopper by applying tight corporate identities to every aspect of their trading activity, both visually and in terms of written slogans.

In the marketing of destinations the use of branding to differentiate what is actually on offer at each destination became far more prominent during the 1980s. The bright and bouncy 'Its Blackpool Magic!', for example, projects a very different image from Eastbourne's gentler visuals and accompanying slogans 'The Warmest Welcome on The South Coast' and 'The Best Resort by a Long Chalk'.

Branding of destinations is not a recent phenomenon. Identities were being created earlier in this century with slogans such as 'Skegness is So Bracing' applied to a visual of a jolly fisherman skipping along the sands.

The contrived name of Llanfairpwllgwyngyllgogerychwyrndrobwllllantysiliogogogoch, a nineteenth-century ruse to impress tourists visiting the island of Ynys Môn in North Wales, still draws the would-be visitor to this day.

Branding, however, is not simply confined to destination marketing. Observation of the major international hotel groups such as Accor, Hilton and Holiday Inns during the early 1990s illustrates clearly the sharpening of brand identities with a view to highlighting different product offerings in a converging market place. The importance of branding is well documented in an article by Travis Dale & Partners.[4]

Theming

In a similar way, themes have been applied increasingly to regions and destinations, either on a short-term or a more permanent basis, to strengthen the image of a destination by association with a particular person, event or manufacture. Thus, for example, Cumbria is associated with Wordsworth, Holland with bulbs in springtime, Lappland with Santa Claus and Bavaria with beer festivals.

The Destination Product

The term 'resort' is often interchanged with destination and is used in the context of both seaside and inland resorts. Many of Britain's seaside resorts, built during the last century to meet the leisure needs of the burgeoning Victorian industrial cities, have suffered a declining image in recent times which in many instances reflects a real decline in terms of infrastructure. With fewer long-stay holidaymakers, suppliers moving out of the business and a lack of investment, a resort can easily begin to look in need of refurbishment. One has only to observe the decline of the traditional seaside pier or the lack of appeal of promenades in so many of Britain's smaller resorts to establish the point. The concept of the product life cycle and its application to seaside resorts in decline has been explored by Cooper and Jackson[5] in the case of the Isle of Man.

Product Development

In any given organisation a major functional role of marketing is product development. In this context, marketing is very much about setting a framework within which certain types of development are encouraged and others not. A strategy of rejuvenation has been adopted by several resorts, but very often on an incremental rather than a sustained basis.

Appropriate development is important. For example, one of Britain's finest Victorian seaside resorts, Llandudno, would wish to resist the development of building along the main North Shore promenade as this would significantly alter its distinctive Edwardian image. In a similar manner, many of the inland spa towns such as Buxton in Derbyshire and Llandrindod Wells in Mid-Wales have sought in recent years to rekindle interest in such matters as the production of spa waters and encouraging the pursuit of healthy activities. As part of this revival strategy there has been increased interest in the restoration of fine Georgian or Victorian buildings for such purposes. These destinations would not, however, be so keen to encourage a Wild West fun park within their heritage areas.

The notion that product development, in terms of product planning and screening, can be applied to a destination is only partially true. A resort might well have a product development strategy, but as there are so many parties involved the process tends to be of an incremental nature. When it comes to the practical application of strategic approaches marketing techniques may also be applied.

It is feasible that the tourism marketeer can influence development by establishing a framework within which other product offerings are assessed as acceptable, or otherwise. For example, tourism officers might well establish a criteria grid to evaluate modified or new product offerings in relation to the background of the resort's overall marketing strategy. The criteria grid as outlined in Table 8.1. illustrates such an approach.

Table 8.1   Criteria grid

Product acceptibility level	Weighting(1)	Score(2) 0 1 2 3 4 5 6 7 8 9 10	Rating((1)x(2))
Idea compatibility*	0.20	/	0.60
Location	0.10	/	0.30
Company past record	0.05	/	0.25
Research into marketing	0.05	/	0.30
Company marketing capability	0.10	/	0.80
Presentation of ideas	0.05	/	0.40
Timescales projected	0.10	/	0.40
Planning constraints	0.15	/	0.45
Environmental Benefits	0.20	/	0.60

Weightings*
In this case, the score is 410, which is a poor rating.

> * How does the attraction or accommodation proposal fit into the overall product strategy for the destination ?
> ** Weightings are often devised by analysing previous and current policy documents and marketing strategies to assess which factors are considered important in relation to others. The process is subjective and is usually a matter of managerial judgement.

The term 'destination', however, means more than a projected image. It is partly tangible as a product offering and includes major components such as:

> ● The physical landscape moulded by humans
> ● The transport system (road, rail, ferries, air)
> ● The accommodation sector
> ● The range of visitor attractions, and so on

These combine to make up the destination, a term which has been widely defined to include major attractions, holiday centres such as Center Parcs and places such as Torbay. In the latter example, the make-up of the product, unlike Center Parcs, is supplied by numerous organisations and companies of varying sizes, resources and differing goals. For those marketing destinations, product development is thus not the domain of one or two product managers, as might be expected, but within the remit of dozens of people, from the small-scale guest house owner seeking to extend his or her premises, to the property developer proposing a new shopping centre complex.

Decline of Seaside Resorts

It is also appropriate to distinguish between the marketing of a destination and the marketing of a region. As mentioned above, a destination refers to a distinct location – possibly a seaside resort, an historic city or a market town. In this sense, the marketeer is accountable for attracting visitors to these clearly definable and delineated locations. A region, in contrast, embodies numerous locations and while being defined in terms of geographical boundaries, might include widely differing characteristics within relatively short distances.

By using a criteria grid, a set of policy guidelines can be established by which physical planning measures may be stipulated. This allows the marketeer to input into what is a complicated and fragmented process. This is particularly necessary as the development of a resort's infrastructure may well be planned wholly on the basis of an overall industrial policy with scant regard for the needs of tourism. For example, a County Council in conjunction with the Department of Transport may propose an inner relief road, on general economic grounds, which would be extremely detrimental to an area of natural beauty or historic interest and therefore be far less attractive to residents and visitors to a resort. Traditionally, cost-benefit techniques have not so far incorporated approaches to environmental impact in any sophisticated way.

Coordination

The second major point about product development is coordination. The tourism marketeer's role is to bring different attractions and accommodation providers together to package new or modified offerings in an acceptable way to the visitor. This can be seen in terms of the built environment, and is often product- rather than market-led where a number of attractions are grouped together in one zone or where accommodation and attraction suppliers locate in close proximity. A good example of this would be the old Covent Garden in London where museums and shops are using old market warehouses, or at Gloucester Docks where a similar scheme is reaching maturity. Complementarity is the key to the success of such schemes – i.e. shops, museums, accommodation and catering providing a suitable overall appeal.

Similarly, individual companies will be screening new projects as an internal company exercise as in any other business sector (i.e. sifting ideas for use of a site, applying a financial appraisal and estimating forecasts of demand and expected revenue). This, as mentioned above, almost certainly involves close liaison with local authority officers to ensure that a development is compatible with key planning documents such as structure or local plans. Center Parcs, for example, go to considerable lengths to locate their holiday centres in areas which are not only viable in terms of visitor catchment but also fit into a local environmental framework.

In summary the major tasks facing those responsible for marketing a destination are:

(1) Product enhancement and new product development
(2) Market development
(3) Promotion of the destination, including the creation of an appropriate destination image

A continuing enhancement of facilities obviously allows a marketeer to seek new markets as well as consolidating mature ones, as the study of The English Riviera illustrates.

The Case

Torbay, lying on the southern coast of Devon, is one of Britain's major seaside resorts with 9.5 million bednights taken per annum, second only to Blackpool in the North West of England. Torbay comprises three key seaside resort towns along an eight-mile stretch of coastline around the bay, each location having a very different character (see Figure 8.1). Brixham is the smallest resort, being a working fishing port with narrow streets and passages threading away from the harbour to old fishermen's cottages and wayside inns. The central quayside, however, is far busier and more commercialised. Paignton is well known as a family resort with safe beaches, parks, a pier and several visitor attractions. Of the three, Torquay is seen as a premier resort of international standing given its scenic backcloth, level of attractions and strong accommodation sector. Having once attracted the gentry in the last century it became more accessible to a mass market with the opening up of the West Country by the Great Western Railway which marketed the area under the banner of the 'English Riviera'.

For the best part of the twentieth century, Torbay has thus been a major UK resort catering for the long-stay holidaymaker enjoying an annual holiday in the warmer south of England. The current estimate of the value of tourism to Torbay is in excess of £200 million per annum, tourism-related businesses providing the major source of employment.

As with so many British resorts trade began to recede in the late 1970s after a peak year in 1977 when 12.7 million bednights were recorded. The reasons suggested for this downward trend experienced by so many UK and northern Europe resorts can be summarised as follows:

- Widening horizons of customers
- Increased availability of competitive package holidays abroad
- Limited marketing activity undertaken by UK resorts

The trend had become established as a pattern for many seaside resorts earlier than Torbay. By the late 1970s, however, Torbay found that businesses were moving out of tourism, especially accommodation providers (Table 8.2).

Figure 8.1   The English Riviera

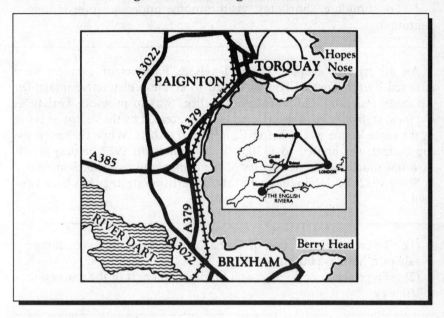

Source: Torbay Tourist Board.

**Table 8.2   Capacity of tourist accommodation in Torbay
(bednight capacity)**

	1986	1987	1988	1989
Brixham	9280	9350	8260	7860
Paignton	26970	26580	26140	24340
Torquay	27360	27330	26270	25600
Total	63610	63260	60670	57810

Source: West Country Tourist Board.

In 1982, The Torbay Tourist Board set about arresting the decline of
the resort, and the following objectives were set:

1. To hold Torbay's share of the traditional long-stay market
2. To encourage new visitor volume by projecting a 'continental-
style' holiday in the UK – i.e. the best possible UK substitute resort
instead of a holiday abroad

3. To penetrate the more affluent South East market
4. To stimulate short-stay visits among upper socio-economic groupings

An advertising agency, Travis Davis & Partners of London were engaged by the Torbay Tourist Board to create a distinctive image for Brixham, Paignton and Torquay. The brief was to promote Torbay as the most stylish English resort area, to be perceived by the visitor as being in the same league as the better Continental resorts. While the advertising budget was limited to £130,000 per annum (in 1982 values) and is now not much more, the success of the campaign is well recognised.

Since 1982 the dominant part of the advertising strategy has been two-fold:

(1)   To create distribution of Torbay's main brochure to encourage sale of a holiday, but also
(2)   To project a new image as a fundamental part of the marketing strategy

The campaign has generated direct brochure responses among potential visitors (see Table 8.3 for a customer profile). The brochure has been restyled with a distinctive palm tree visual, the words 'The English Riviera' and the use of three vibrant colours. This robust branding device (see Figure 8.2) has been maintained throughout, and is likely to become one of the 'classics' in years to come, having already won over twenty awards within the advertising business. In the early days of 1982 it was a marked departure from the standard approach to tourism destination guides. It has been argued that by declaring the image the Torbay Tourist Board wished to attain, appropriate development has followed. In most destinations, the reverse is true: i.e. development precedes image building.

In 1986, the English Riviera won, alongside another resort, an English Tourist Board-sponsored 'Resort 2000' competition and received grant aid to establish a Tourist Development Action Programme (TDAP), an initiative to assess and market the potential of the resort through a series of action plans. Financed by Torbay Borough Council, the English Tourist Board, Devon County Council and the West Country Tourist Board the TDAP had similar objectives to those mentioned above but with a remit to stimulate further the development of the resort as well as the market place. This was to be resourced by a partnership of funding from the private and public sector. Table 8.5 lists a number of key projects developed during recent years. Despite a few setbacks the TDAP

Table 8.3   Characteristics of British tourists to the West Country

	1985	1987	1988	(%)
Age group				
16–24	20	20	16	
25–34	21	20	23	
35–44	17	16	20	
45–54	18	13	12	
55–64	13	16	15	
65plus	12	16	13	
Economic status				
AB	28	28	32	
C1	26	28	26	
C2	30	26	26	
DE	16	17	17	
Mode of transport				
Car	76	78	NA	
Train	7	8	NA	
Bus	6	3	NA	
Coach Tour	4	4	NA	
Hired Car	2	2	NA	
Other	6	5	NA	
Region of origin				
North	1	2	NA	
Yorks/Humberside	4	4	NA	
North West	7	5	NA	
East Midlands	7	6	NA	
West Midlands	12	12	NA	
East Anglia	3	2	NA	
London/South East	35	38	NA	
South West	27	25	NA	
Wales	3	4	NA	
Scotland	2	1	NA	

Source: *Devon Tourism Review 1989*, as adapted from the West Country Tourist Board data 1989.

has established an air of confidence with regard to investment in the resort and the accommodation sector has stabilised, with fewer concerns leaving the business. In fact, it is the view of many that the image success has led to the development of the resort rather than the reverse – i.e. by declaring the image.

Figure 8.2   The English Riviera brand image

Source: Torbay Tourist Board.

The medium used has been predominantly small black and white adverts placed in a variety of newspapers and magazines, backed initially by a limited television campaign and then subsequently by posters using Adshell illuminated bus shelter locations sited mainly in London. Table 8.4 illustrates the take-up of *The English Riviera Guide* in the early part of 1990, 200,000 of which are published for distribution annually. Overall, the cost per response has been minimal, making it a rewarding campaign.

Table 8.4   Enquiries for English Riviera Guide January–May 1990

Following a schedule of placing small black and white adverts in these publications in November and December:

Daily newspapers
Daily Mirror	2900
Sun	3100

Sunday newspapers
News of The World	5300
Sunday Mirror	4200
Sunday People	4200
Mail on Sunday	800
Sunday Express	400

Weeklies
Radio Times	12000
TV Times	11000
Woman	5000
Woman's Own	5400
Woman's Weekly	5600
Woman's Realm	3600

Monthlies
Readers Digest	2000
Woman and Home	700

Other guides
England Holidays	2500	
West Country	1300	
Cream of Devon	500	
Coastwise	300	
Let's Go	200	
Editorial Coverage	700	(Known responses from articles)
Other Responses	13000	(50% Tourist Information Centre enquiries, others unident.)
Total	84700	

Source: Torbay Tourist Board. Data amended to maintain confidentiality.

Table 8.5   Product development on Torbay 1986–1990

Major non-accommodation developments:

• The English Riviera Centre
A £15 million Torbay Council based development of conference, exhibition and leisure complex opened in 1987.

• Torquay Marina
A private sector development within the Council's Torquay Harbour and associated waterside land use. The 600-berth marina with speciality shopping complex in the conserved pavilion is now fully open.

• Quaywest
An outdoor water park (Aquaventureland) and family entertainment centre opened in 1988 by Rush and Tomkin Leisure. Future uncertain, but further expansion not foreseen in the short term.

• Fleet Walk Shopping Centre
Estimated £30 million 'heritage styled' but modern shopping complex, in central Torquay linking the older shopping zone to the harbour.

• Brixham Marina
The first phase opened in 1989 with a 600-berth marina and initial waterside apartments. This has recently been taken over by the owners of Torquay marina. There are plans for more waterside apartments and other waterside facilities adjacent to the marina. Nearby is a new visitor attraction – 'Perils of The Deep'

Other Schemes:
In 1989, Paignton Zoo was revitalised with the opening of a Rhinoceros House and improved catering facilities. Torquay Leisure Hotels have built an indoor bowls facililty of international standard.

Dozens of smaller-scale schemes such as improving the beaches and seafront, repaving, resigning, etc. are being carried out and the accommodation sector is investing a record amount in upgrading property.

Source: Torbay Tourist Board (1990).

The Torbay Tourist Board has without a doubt created a strong identity for the resort, and has consolidated its position in the long-stay market, a volume market which is valued. Given that this market, in UK terms, is still in decline, there is a need to look more urgently at other markets.

The Task

You have been appointed recently as a junior tourism executive reporting to the Director of The Torbay Tourist Board.

Your first major task is to prepare a draft report which outlines ways in which new markets can be attracted to the English Riviera Include in the report a smaller section which suggests further improvements to Torbay in terms of product development commensurate with Torbay's new image

References

1. V.T.C. Middleton, *Seaside Resorts* (English Tourist Board, *Insights*, 1989).
2. A.V. Seaton 'Symbolism, Structural Branding and Representation in Tourism Choices', Conference Paper, Tourism Research into the 1990s (Durham University, 1990).
3. N. Telisman-Kosuta 'Tourist Destination Image', S.F. Witt, and L. Moutinho, *Tourism Marketing and Management Handbook* (Prentice-Hall, 1989).
4. Travis Dale & Partners, *Advertising The English Riviera* (English Tourist Board, *Insights*, 1989).
5. C.P. Cooper and S. Jackson, *Destination Life Cycle: the Isle of Man Case Study* (Annals of Tourism Research, 1989).

A useful backgroun history is provided by I. Ousby, *The Englishman's England* (Cambridge University Press, 1990).

The author gratefully acknowledges the assistance of the Torbay Tourist Board in the preparation of this case. Certain aspects have been amended to maintain confidentiality of data.

88

9 Granada Studios Tours: You Won't Believe it 'Till You See it!

Objectives

(a) To discuss the issue of seasonality and management of demand
(b) To evaluate promotional campaign techniques
(c) To understand the importance of visitor care at attractions

Management of Demand

Controlling demand is one of the major tasks facing marketeers in tourism. This case study illustrates how one attraction, Granada Studios Tours at Manchester, has approached the management of demand, and in particular has sought to increase business during traditional troughs. Granada Studios Tours, as with many visitor attractions, also has a capacity constraint: the attraction can physically accommodate only a given number of customers in any one day. The case also highlights the importance of the 'visitor experience', and how staff are vital in this process.

Seasonality

Most attractions have to meet the challange of seasonality – i.e. the erratic pattern of demand throughout the year. For most tourism-related businesses the main season extends from Easter to late October, and for many attractions 95 per cent of their trade is catered for during these months, the peak of peaks being from late July to the first week of September. This may not always be the case. In certain instances – such as resorts serving the winter sports market, say, for skiing and tobogganing, a mirror image applies.

Accommodation providers in traditional tourist resorts will still be able to sell their facilities several times over during the summer holiday period, even though the solidity of the holiday pattern prevalent a decade ago is weakening. On the other hand, business-based hotels in urban areas, which are often oversubscribed during the week, have difficulty in selling bednights at weekends. The issue of seasonality at different times of the year, week and day is one which has been often addressed. The response has tended to be two-pronged;

(1) **The use of pricing strategies to regulate demand**. This can be illustrated in terms of tariffs for letting cottages or boats, for example, where the same facility is priced high during the peak season and differentially at other times according to estimated demand.

Consider British Rail InterCity, which uses pricing as a mechanism to regulate demand. On the busiest trains to and from London and provincial cities premium pricing is applied as demand tends to be fairly price-inelastic. If a business person has an appointment at 1100 he or she will pay a higher price to be on the early morning train to the Capital. On the other hand, when seats are available at mid-day, those with less rigid time scales will be able to buy a journey at a much reduced fare. The same applies to hotels. A room which sells for £75 on Monday to Thursday evenings will lie empty on other nights if not offered at a preferential rate to a different market. The concept of 'perishability' makes flexible pricing so important: the product cannot be stored as can many other goods which can be warehoused until demand picks up. Empty seats or rooms today cannot be stockpiled for tomorrow.

(2) **Promotional Activity which stimulates the use of spare capacity**.
As well as pricing attractively to stimulate demand at off-peak times, there has been a concerted campaign in recent years to change the image of late Autumn, Winter and early Spring from being quiet, uninspiring times. Tourist Boards, hotels and resorts have

increasingly begun to market the 'shoulder months' as imaginative, fun times when taking a holiday without the crowds allows the visitor to get more from a visit. Hence images of log fires, woodland hues and indoor pursuits are encouraged.

More enterprises have been encouraged to open throughout the year by Tourist Boards. Blackpool pioneered this approach in the 1920s with the now famous Blackpool Illuminations. The peak of the year for the resort in terms of visitor numbers is now late October-early November rather than August. Others have attempted similar initiatives, but not on such a bold scale. Visitor attractions have tended to concentrate on an intensive period of activity around the Christmas holidays. Many of the steam leisure railways, having previously closed for the entire winter, now reopen for two to three weeks to offer rides to meet Father Christmas, to partake of a glass of sherry or lemonade and a mince pie. But what about the other months ?

'Operation Off Peak', a tourism supplier-based scheme, has attempted to generate creative ideas to stimulate demand through promotional activity at times of limited demand and there have been a series of outstanding successes. Great City Breaks, outlined in Case 7, is one example, generating thousands of trips during the traditionally quieter months. Lincoln Fair in the month of December, and the Viking Festival in York during February are other examples of off-peak activities which have achieved surprising results.

For most attractions, the opportunities presented by spread and seasonality require a three-fold analysis:

(1) Which customers can be persuaded to visit at off-peak times (however defined) – i.e. a degree of market analysis and segmentation?
(2) Does the attraction require any modification at these times – i.e. product analysis?
(3) How can the targeted segments be persuaded to visit – i.e. the promotional mix?

For example, the Alton Towers theme park in Staffordshire assessed that the potential for attracting people during winter months could be realised by arranging special indoor events around the Festive season and promoting the beautiful gardens during late Autumn and into Spring even though the theme rides are not in operation at these times. This required very little product modification but a distinctly different campaign targeted mainly to an older market looking for a good day out in the beautiful gardens rather than a series of rides with twists and thrills.

Promotional Campaigns

The case study also focuses on the need for short-term action pro-grammes to meet the specific requirements of the market place, bearing in mind the seasonality of an attraction. In this case study, the key task is to create a promotional campaign to stimulate demand for Granada Studios Tours during two months of very low demand. The marketing tools available within the promotional mix are outlined in Figure 9.1.

Table 9.1   The promotional mix

ABOVE THE LINE:

Advertisements	Paid for adverts in newspapers, magazines, commercial radio, etc. Displays on poster sites, buses, etc. at commercial rates

BELOW THE LINE:

Public Relations	Unpaid media coverage of events, stories, people associated with a company – all media Internal communications to keep staff informed, advised and motivated
Sponsorship	Financial support of an event or promotion in return for identity and coverage in aspects of publicity material
Publicity	Production of leaflets, brochures, posters giftware, etc.
Personal selling	Use of marketing personnel to visit customers such as presentations to groups, etc.
Merchandising	Display of publicity material, souvenirs with a message in shop and other outlets
Sales promotion	Incentives and added-value promotions such as vouchers, coupons, discounts, etc.
Exhibitions	Three dimensional stand displays at trade markets, etc. Direct marketing Direct contact with the customer mainly by phone or mail.
Word of mouth	Usually by staff and customers to others.

The major problems confronting the marketeer when implementing promotional campaigns relate to sequencing and control, both in terms of time and budget. When adopting a multi-faceted campaign there might be three or four organisations involved and campaign coordination is vital to bring the initiatives together at the right time. For example, a direct response company might be organising a mailing campaign, a PR agency media liaison, and a design studio for the production of a leaflet for a campaign, while you, as the member of staff coordinating the campaign, are briefing in-house staff about the sales promotion incentives being offered. The adoption of achievable targets and realistic schedules with an allocation of time for slippage when a campaign involves outside agencies should form the basis of a sound campaign.

The Case

'You won't believe it 'till you see it!' is the slogan used to publicise Granada Studios Tours at Manchester, part of the Granada Group. which has a strong business mission evidenced in the Group Aims and Values set out in Figure 9.1.

Figure 9.1   Granada Group Aims and Values document

The aim of Granada Group is to grow stronger by developing leisure and service businesses and so achieve above-average returns for its shareholders. This will be done by innovation, investment, acquisition and restructuring in four business areas – Rental and Retail, Television, Leisure and Business Services.

In pursuing these aims, Granada will adhere to certain values. Granada is committed to ensuring customer satisfaction and loyalty by providing a mix of quality, service and price of which it can be proud. Granada staff will be treated fairly and will have opportunities to develop their abilities. Granada will play its part in the local and national communities in which it operates. In the long run, these values will enhance the return to shareholders and they will not, therefore, be abandoned in response to short term pressures.

Source: *Granada Company Report*, 1989.

Figure 9.2 Management structure of Granada Group

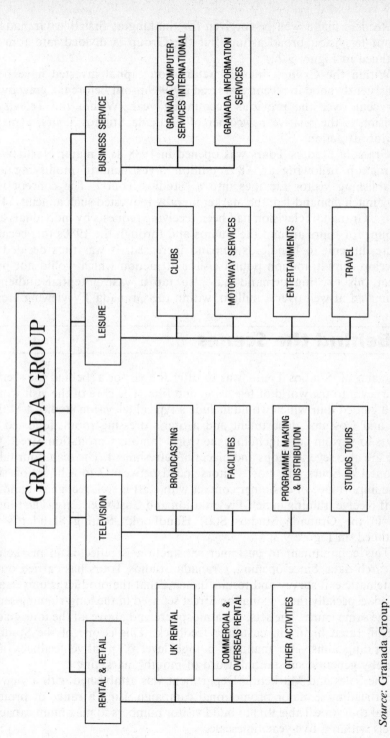

Source: Granada Group.

Readers might well be forgiven for thinking at first that Granada is about television broadcasting, but the Group is divided into four as outlined in Figure 9.2.

Within the Group, financial returns on capital invested have been consistently good in recent years and in 1989 profit before tax grew by 15 per cent over the previous accounting year. Within the Television division is the relative newcomer of Granada Studios Tours, a major visitor attraction.

Granada Studios Tours was opened in 1988 as a major North West attraction following an £8½ million investment in modifying and establishing visitor facilities into a 'Studios Tours'. The concept was very much demand-led; the market literally requested such a facility. For years, Granada Television had been receiving requests by individuals and groups for tours around the studios and through the 1980s this became more difficult to handle as demand increased. It was thus decided to develop a multi-million pound visitor attraction which would not only meet this existing demand but also tap a vast potential audience, estimated at well over a million, within the Granada TV viewing area.

Behind the Scenes

The aim of 'Studios Tours' was to offer the visitor a 'behind the scenes' journey into the world of television and film. The core of the visit would be a guided tour which would include a typical television studio, a Make-up and Costume department and a Star's dressing room, followed by visits to various sets, including the world-famous Coronation Street. On site are also several shops and places of refreshment. The main tour takes about 1½ hours and most visitors spend between 3 to 4 hours on site. The importance of customer contact with staff is well recognised and all staff receive training in Self-Presentation and Customer Care. The tone is set in the Granada Studios Staff Handbook, 'Setting Standards' as outlined, in Figure 9.3.

This commitment to customer satisfaction is reflected in marketing research data. Since opening, Granada Studios Tours has carried out a systematic exit survey and results indicate that the product is universally loved, especially the Coronation Street set used in the long-running series of the same name. The sets, the atmosphere and above all the tour guides are all rated highly in customer feedback. This is one of the Studio's overriding aims – to maintain a high level of positive feedback and thereby generate substantial 'word of mouth' marketing.

The Sales and Marketing Department was established with a view to spearheading a major promotional campaign using a range of promotional tools (see Table 9.1) to build visitor numbers to maximum capacity levels within a five-year timescale.

Figure 9.3 'Setting Standards', Granada Studios Staff Handbook

"Performing the Role"

"The First Impression is the Lasting Impression"

Every Guest arrives at Granada Studios Tour with high expectations for their day out.

Whether you are a Car Park Attendant, Litter Picker, or Tour Guide, you are all, at some time or other, likely to meet our Guests. So remember, no matter how many times a day and every day you are asked the same question, it is actually the first time – for our Guests.

Your uniform makes you look the part but only when you can project the image of Granada Studios Tour in everything you say and do will you have really mastered the role.

First you will need confidence. The Self-Presentation and Customer Care Training are designed as foundations to your Guest Relations Skills and will provide the necessary confidence.

Both your confidence and skills will increase each day, but our Guests will not know a new cast member from an experienced one, so being new is never an excuse – if you do not know the answer to the question then take the Guest to someone who does, when you listen to the answer you are rehearsing for the next time.

Act professionally, acknowledge each Guest immediately with a smile, and then give your full attention.

Apologise for any delays and always use proper titles such as Sir and Madam. If you are accepting a cheque or credit card use their full name, "Thank you Mr Smith".

It is these details our Guests will remember most and use as recommendations to their families and friends.

Keeping in Character.

The Granada Studios Tour professional does not bring their personal life to work and they certainly never discuss it in front of a Guest – it ruins the illusion we have all worked so hard to create.

Complaints – How to deal with them.

WE hope there won't be any but...Remain polite at all times, and remember *behaviour breeds behaviour*.

Play the scene with your utmost professional ability –

1. Do not take things seriously – if you are unsympathetic the situation grows worse

2. Apologise for any inconvenience and find a Supervisor/Manager or take the Guest to Guest Relations, they will deal further with the matter.

3. Always put yourself in the Guests position, their expectations are high and must not be disappointed.

Source: Granada Group.

A Sales and Marketing Manager was appointed to head up a small team with the following remit:

> (1) To maintain the highest quality visitor attraction in Britain
> (2) To establish and retain high customer satisfaction levels
> (3) To maximise revenue by managing demand for the attraction throughout the year
> (4) To achieve a satisfactory return on investment

The market was segmented into three distinct groups

> (a) **Individuals**: the main market including small groups of friends and relatives visiting Granada Studios Tours on a casual basis. Predominantly C1, C2 and DE socio-economic grouping, and mainly coming from a 100-mile radius of the attraction.
> (b) **Groups**: ranging from school parties to retired groups, with a propensity to travel further distances than individuals
> (c) **Corporate Hospitality**: a much smaller market with very different needs; mainly commercial companies rewarding staff with a special visit or as part of a conference activity being held in the Manchester area.

Within an estimated promotional budget of approximately £250,000 per annum the tendency has been to concentrate on 'Above the Line' activity as outlined below:

	£
Advertisements in local and regional papers	160,000
Publicity Material:one multi-purpose, full-colour leaflet	25,000
Direct Response: mailing to groups throughout the country with some tele sales back-up	30,000
Public Relations: targeted to groups and individuals	10,000
Exhibitions/Trade Fairs	10,000

This promotional effort has two key objectives:

> (a) To increase awareness of Granada Studios as an entertaining destination
> (b) To convert this awareness into actual trips to the Studios

The major problem confronting Granada Studios, however, is how to cope with peaks and troughs. Demand is peaked throughout the day with most arrivals occurring between 1100 and 1300 hours. Furthermore, weekends and Wednesday are far busier than Tuesday, Thursday and Monday. Friday is always the day of least demand. Granada Studios has a maximum capacity of 4000 guests in any one day. On a warm Bank Holiday the major task is to dampen demand for there is insufficient capacity to handle all comers. On the other hand, a quiet Tuesday in January is not likely to attract a fifth of maximum capacity (see Table 9.2 for an estimate of seasonal demand). This issue of seasonality and spreading demand has been discussed on several occasions by the marketing team and a number of measures tried on a small-scale basis. Further action is required to meet targets.

Table 9.2   Estimated peaks and troughs: Granada Studios Tours

Visitors	JAN	FEB	MAR	APR	MAY	JUN	JUL	AUG	SEP	OCT	NOV	DEC
100,000								●				
80,000							●					
60,000						●			●			
40,000					●							
40,000				●						●		
20,000		●	●								●	●
20,000	●											
0												

Table 9.2 reflects a generalised pattern of demand, but is not based on real data.

The Task

You have been brought in by Granada Studios Tours as a marketing executive from a local marketing consultancy to devise a promotional campaign to increase off-peak demand in Winter. The budget specified is between £20,000 and £30,000. Two specific requirements have been included in the brief:

(1) Make suggestions for spreading demand throughout the day and during the week
(2) Outline a promotional campaign to attract 20 per cent more visitors in December and January (the weakest months) than in the previous year

Reference

A. Jefferson and L. Lickorish, *Marketing Tourism: A Practical Guide* (Longman, 1988).

The author gratefully acknowledges the assistance of Granada Studios Tours in the preparation of this case. The data have been amended to retain confidentiality of material.

10 Trusthouse Forte: Business Guarantee

Objectives

(a) To evaluate customer service provision
(b) To prepare a specific action plan
(c) To understand hotel marketing

Quality Service

Product differentiation through the provision of quality service has become an increasingly important dimension of marketing in tourism. It is a concept adopted by many of the hotel chains competing in a world market. The concept simply does not mean the addition of more luxury items in hotels, with a consequent price increase to the customer: the market is too sensitive to sustain such an approach. It is about offering a consistent, value-added service to the guest without incurring heavily increased costs.

The matter is particularly pertinent when dealing with the business travel market, and Trusthouse Forte, along with other hotel groups, have monitored and upgraded their product accordingly. Within the UK, Trusthouse Forte (THF) is predominant in its supply of quality provision for the business sector, given its geographical spread and strong representation in London and the major provincial cities. The case raises the question of service levels expected by the business traveller and the maintenance of quality standards within this context.

Business Travel

The business travel market, as one would expect, is the mainstay of many accommodation providers. The spend of the business traveller is usually higher than guests staying for leisure purposes, and the pattern of travel is nowhere near as seasonal as in other segments. The market is recognised by all sectors of the the tourism business, and in recent years several airlines and British Rail have established travel clubs offering additional benefits for frequent travellers.

Hotels such as Novotel, Stakis and THF have offered incentives to business people staying on a regular basis. The incentive usually comes in the form of a discount, but also includes a variety of additional bonuses such as reservations, better-quality rooms and so on. Segmentation has also extended to catering specifically for female executives in several hotels. For example, Crest Hotels (now part of THF) were innovators in establishing Lady Crest rooms with additional facilities for female business guests.

Table 10.1   Service quality – expressive service quality

Factor	Comment
Reliability	Consistent performance, getting things done right the first time
Responsiveness	Willingness of employees to provide service
Competence	Having the necessary skills and knowledge to undertake the task competently
Access	Approachability, body language
Courtesy	Politeness and respect, consideration and friendliness
Communication	Keeping customers informed without using jargon
Credibility	Honesty and believability
Security	Minimising risk and danger
Understanding	Making an effort to know the customer's needs
Tangibles	Physical evidence such as dress, appearance

Source: Based on the work of A. Parasuraman, V.A. Zeithaml and L.L. Bery 'A Conceptual Model of Service Quality and its Implications for Future Research', *Journal of Marketing*, 4 (1985).
This formed the basis of further work on the Servqual customer service model.

Quality

The key to satisfying the business market has been partly about establishing favourable corporate tariffs, but equally about raising quality standards. The establishment of standards pervades all aspects of hotel provision, from the decor of the restaurant to the facilities provided in each room, the cleaning routines, and the computerised reservation system. Above all else, staff are the driving force of a quality approach, conviviality being a crucial aspect, as summarised in Table 10.1. This approach relies on judicious recruitment, training, and motivation of management and staff. It is important to recruit staff who have the right frame of mind, who are flexible and can develop as a job grows, and who can in the process build self-esteem and competence.

Obviously, management's role is important. Involvement is essential at every stage and the design of systems and procedures to meet customer requirements is a fundamental step in establishing quality standards. It is difficult to evaluate the direct benefits of such an approach, but readers might like to consider an article by Walker and Salameh[1] about the returns from a quality approach in the USA hotel sector.

Figure 10.1   Tangibles–intangibles matrix

		TANGIBLE	INTANGIBLE
		Quality matrix – Hotel provision Characteristics of the experience	
PHYSICAL		The product Facilitating goods Information processes	Atmosphere Esthetics Feelings Comfort
INTERPERSONAL	Nature of the contact	Actions Process Speed Script Corrective action	Warmth Friendliness Care Service

Adapted from Lockwood and Jones, 1988.

Lockwood and Jones.[2] in discussing the combination of tangibles and intangibles in quality provision present the matrix in Figure 10.1.

Note that the quadrants in Figure 10.1 are not equal, which is a reflection of the priority weighting between different components. For example, the Interpersonal/Tangible dimension is more important than the Interpersonal/Intangible one. The criteria listed in this matrix form the basis of most quality standards programmes in the accommodation sector.

Furthermore, as the market place has become more competitive, the main contenders have reviewed their approach to the business travel market and reformulated their offering to this market segment, some more successfully than others. This case is about how THF has approached the business traveller market by establishing quality standards in their service offering.

The Case

THF has been in existence as a major UK-based hotel group since the 1960s. It has a reputation for being a quality provider of hotel accommodation, maintaining an image analogous to British Airways, Jaguar, Marks and Spencer or Sainsburys. The company is certainly undisputed UK market leader in terms of hotel provision, and is also important on an international dimension, particularly in the USA where it has 437 hotels, mainly under the Travelodge banner. It is currently seeking to develop its international portfolio. THF also has a much wider portfolio than hotel provision, which gives it a strong corporate position in the the hotel and catering business sector, as can be seen from Tables 10.2 and 10.3.

The current company philosophy is projected in Figure 10.2 and the long-term nature of these general mission statements gives an indication of the THF group's approach to the market place. The financial results of the company have been strong during the past decade as evidenced in the sales, profit and capital expenditure figures outlined in Figure 10.3.

One of the company's strengths has been its ability to maintain a wide range of hotels, both historic and modern, which have genuine character. Although levels of service are designed to be high in any THF property the hotels are grouped into various categories according to facilities available and are marketed as such. Thus, the Swan Hotel at Grasmere in the Lake District or the Saracen's Head at Southwell, Nottinghamshire will be marketed primarily to leisure travellers because of their location and size. In contrast, the 5-star flagship Grosvenor House Hotel in Park Lane has a distinctly up-market clientele and other 4-star houses in the

Table 10.2   THF portfolio

	U.K.	Continental Europe	North America	Rest of the World	Total
Hotels	265	30	437	11	743
Rooms	23,871	5,591	34,676	2,486	66,624
Health & Fitness Clubs	44	–	–	–	44
Sales Offices	3	7	7	5	22
Flight Catering Kitchens	20	4	1	-	25
Airport Shops	74	–	–	–	74
Catering Contracts	2,850	926	520	122	4,418
Public Restaurants	995	–	–	–	995
Motorway Service Areas	23	–	–	–	23
Supply Depots	8	–	–	–	8

Source: THF.

group such as the Albany at Birmingham or the Post House at Middlesbrough seek mainstream business travellers to meet their occupancy target levels.

Figure 10.2   Company philosophy document

To increase profitability and earnings per share each year in order to encourage investment and to improve and expand the business.

To give complete customer satisfaction by efficient and courteous service, with value for money

To support managers and their staff in using personal initiative to improve the profit and quality of their operations whilst observing the Company's policies.

To provide good working conditions and to maintain effective communications at all levels to develop better understanding and assist decision making.

To ensure no discrimination against sex, race, colour or creed.

To train, develop and encourage promotion within the company based on merit and ability.

To act with integrity and to maintain a proper sense of responsibility towards the public.

To recognise the importance of each and every employee.

Source: THF.

With such a wide range of hotels offering different features and facilities, a problem arises about customer expectations and levels of service available. THF has always been aware of the need to establish management and staff training programmes which enhance customer service skills regardless of the market segment, size of hotel and level of facility.

Figure 10.3 Sales, profits and capital expenditure

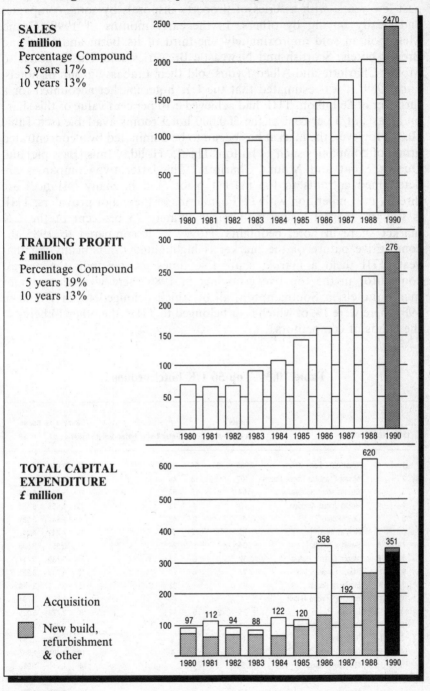

SALES
£ million
Percentage Compound
  5 years 17%
10 years 13%

TRADING PROFIT
£ million
Percentage Compound
  5 years 19%
10 years 13%

**TOTAL CAPITAL
EXPENDITURE**
£ million

☐ Acquisition

▨ New build,
   refurbishment
   & other

Source: THF.

The hotel market place can only be described as very fluid during the past few years, with a series of property disposals by some companies and steady buying by others. In the early months of 1990, Grand Metropolitan sold approximately one-third of its Berni and Chef and Brewer hotels, Scottish and Newcastle Breweries sold Thistle hotels to Mount Charlotte and Allied Lyons sold their Embassy group of hotels.

In 1989, it was estimated that the UK hotel market accounted for a turnover of £6 billion. THF had achieved a 10 per cent value of this share on a basis of 5 per cent of the 500,000 hotel rooms available (see Table 10.3). However, the market has begun to be dominated by a concentrated group of companies such as Hilton, Thistle, Holiday Inns (Bass plc) and Queens Moat and Mount Charlotte. The latter two companies are determined entrants to the market place, and in many instances are directly in competition with THF. In terms of the major providers, THF is still the market leader with approximately 25 per cent of the UK market share in hotel bednights. However, if compared to 1985 the competitive nature of the market is highlighted dramatically. In that year, THF held a market share five times greater than the nearest competitor in the top five grouping: in 1980 there were three major quality hotels in Southampton, all of which belonged to THF and in 1989 there were 18, of which four belonged to THF, the other 14 being in the hands of competitors.

Table 10.3   Top 50 UK hotel groups

1990	1989	Group	Hotels in UK	5-star	4-star	3-star	2-star	1-star	Lodges	Not listed	Rooms in UK	Rooms in '89
1	1	Trusthouse Forte Hotels	265	3	39	123	25		12	63	23,843	24,157
2	2	Mount Charlotte Thistle Hotels	102		15	46	1	1		39	13,787	9,053
3	3	Queens Moat Houses	94	1	15	52	1			25	9,061	6,948
4	4	Hilton United Kingdom	33	1	4	13				15	6,658	6,455
5	5	Crest Hotels	49		2	43				4	5,641	5,581
6	7	Holiday Inns	20		12	2				6	4,242	4,042
7	8	Swallow Hotels	34		5	26				5	3,856	3,696
8	9	Mecca Leisure Hotels	52		3	13	3			33	3,788	3,411
9	10	Stakis Hotels & Inns	27		4	11				12	3,257	3,293
?	11	Embassy Hotels	41		3	33	2			3	3,153	3,140
10	13	Imperial London Hotels	7							7	2,803	2,794
11	12	De Vere Hotels	25	2	6	14				3	2,772	3,025
12	18	Baron Hotels & Leisure	23			5	1			17	2,380	1,631
13	14	Rank Hotels	6	1	3	1				1	2,234	2,234
14	15	Crown Hotels	25		2	4	1			18	2,201	1,387
15	15	Metropole Hotels	5	1						4	1,941	1,936
16	16	Copthorne Hotels	8		4	2				2	1,924	1,778
17	17	Novotel UK	12			11				1	1,879	1,726

18	30	Edwardian Hotels	9		1	1				7	1,766	1,140
19	23	Friendly Hotels	15			4	2			9	1,534	1,408
20	24	Toby Hotels	48			9	8	1		30	1,444	1,389
21	20	Sheraton Hotels	5	1						4	1,439	1,443
22	19	International Hotels Corporation	4	2	2						1,438	1,446
23=	21	North British Trust Hotels	17							17	1,424	1,436
23=	22	Berni and Chef & Brewer Hotels	69			1	33	9		26	1,424	1,413
25	27	Lansbury Hotels	37		1	21	10			5	1,423	1,279
26	31	Firum Hotels	3		1					2	1,402	1,103
27	28	Butlin's Holiday Hotels	5							5	1,313	1,268
28	38	Park Hotels (GB)	9			1				8	1,190	875
29	26	Ramada International	4	2	1					1	1,141	1,347
30	33	Britannia Hotels	4							4	1,108	1,077
31	46	HC Inns	9		1	1				7	1,092	607
32	35	Sarva Hotels	6		1	2				3	1,007	989
33	39	Country Club Hotels	10		2	5				3	964	798
34	45	Granada Lodge Hotels	22			2			12	8	951	621
35	36	Penta Hotels	2		1					1	930	930
36	37	Seymour's Hotels	5			1				4	893	893
37	–	Principal Hotels	13			5	1			7	875	436
38	32	CG Hotels	6							6	872	1,100
39	44	Hotel Ibis UK	5				1			4	844	626
40	47	Resort Hotels	24			6	4			14	844	603
41	–	Beefeater Travel Inns	19						4	15	747	270
42	42	Express Leisure	8							8	737	649
43	40	Savoy Hotels	5	4	1						700	708
44	–	Royal Crown Hotels	13			5				8	690	200
45	41	Scottish Highland Hotels	9		2	6	1				654	653
46	–	Compass Hotels	9			5				4	640	505
47	34	Penguin Hotel Group	6			2				4	603	1,005
48	49	Modern Hotel Group	5							5	600	552
49	50	Brend Hotels	9		4	4	1				555	540
50	–	County Inns	21				5	1		15	488	75
Total:			1,262	15	136	481	100	12	28	490	128,911	120,850

*Total bedrooms for last year's Top 50.
Source: *Caterer and Hotelkeeper* (5 April 1990).

The main competitors as at April 1990 are shown in Table 10.3. In June 1990 THF secured Crest Hotels from Bass plc, an opportunity to extend the range of middle-market hotels, increase geographical coverage and remove one source of major competition in recent years.

This strategic move also meant that the management team have had to consider brand positioning more closely in the middle market, an exercise which had already been undertaken with respect to THF's luxury hotels at one end of the market and its Travelodges at the other.

Business Sector

Above all, THF realised that the business sector would become increasingly critical in terms of holding market share and revenue. While business people amount to only 30 per cent of all guests, they account for double that in revenue terms. Furthermore, patterns of business travel have begun to change discernibly during recent years. For example, in 1980 business meetings, seminars, etc. were booked well in advance and with a regularity that could be predicted and planned for more readily. By 1990 the pattern had changed, with the majority of bookings being made late and with an increasing number of business guests arriving on the day of the overnight stay. Each hotel had been offering a series of specified rates to different customers from a range of previously negotiated deals on a local or national basis. Bookings could be made through a central reservation system, business travel houses or agencies or direct to the hotels concerned. At busy times, demand was outstripping supply at many hotels, causing resentment among regular customers.

Research undertaken by the company showed that business guests had a distinct profile in terms of usage. They booked at least 20 stays per annum, spent an average of 2 to 3 nights per booking and probably spent an estimated £5500 to £7000 per annum with the hotel group. Internal research also indicated that the less frequent business visitor had similar expectations to the regular guest, which could be summarised as follows:

- An expectation that he or she will be booked into a chosen hotel at a given location, regardless of a short lead time for the booking
- That the type of room required will be available
- That booking will be easy, flexible and fast
- That there will be a consistency and reliability in approach
- That a business discount for regular use will be available to him or her as an individual or to the customer's company

---

Thus, in summary, the business guest had become far more demanding in that he or she wanted guaranteed service in return for loyalty and also favoured a degree of recognition and a bit of style as well as a discount.

Given this, the THF marketing team, including those responsible for Quality Assurance, were given the task of establishing a new branded product directed at the business guest with the following four objectives:

1. To differentiate through branding the product offering from other Hotel Group provisions
2. To present both a powerful and easily understood promotion
3. To establish a competitive and attractive corporate scheme on a worldwide basis
4. To deliver what THF promises to deliver in a consistent and quality manner

To quote the Marketing Director, the product 'Business Guarantee' would be recognised as a 'dedicated first class service guaranteeing priority across Trusthouse Forte hotels worldwide'.

The Task

As a project manager working on the scheme, you have been asked to prepare notes for a presentation to the Marketing Director and Quality Assurance Manager outlining possible solutions to the following questions:

- What levels of customer service should we offer the regular business traveller using the new scheme ?
- How should we advise and consult our hotel management staff about the scheme when we have the core package ready to promote?

References

1. J.R. Walker and T.T. Salameh, 'The Q.A. Payoff', *The Cornell Hotel and Restaurant Administration Quarterly* (February 1990) pp. 57–9.
2. A. Lockwood and P.L.M. Jones *The Management of Hotel Operations* (Cassell, 1988).

You may find the following texts valuable for your understanding of hotel marketing.

M. Greene, *Marketing Hotels and Restaurants into The 1990s* (Heinemann, 1987).
S. Medlik, *The Business of Hotels* (Heinemann, 1989).

The author gratefully acknowledges the assistance of Trusthouse Forte in the preparation of this case. Certain aspects have been amended to maintain confidentiality of data.

11 The Peak District National Park: The Upper Derwent

Objectives

(a) To understand the practical aspects of demand management and demarketing
(b) To be aware of the problems of mass tourism

A Green Decade?

The 1990s has been heralded as the 'green decade' where the discussion about sustainable or 'gentle' tourism will increasingly be translated into policy and action programmes. Figure 11.1 from *Tourism Enterprise* illustrates the point well. The discussion about whether the concept of 'green tourism' is applicable in certain circumstances only and is no real solution to the problems generated by mass tourism is a source of considerable debate.[1] Whatever the outcome, the focus of attention is now more about managing demand than creating it.[2] For a number of areas within the UK such as Stratford upon Avon and York, however, the management of visitor numbers has been a matter of reality for years. The problem of saturation also exists in several countryside areas especially in some of the National Parks such as the Lake District and the Peak parks, two of the most visited places in Europe, if not in the world.

Managing Demand

Managing demand is a very sensitive issue when it comes to conserving and improving the very environment which the visitor seeks to enjoy without introducing total restraint. This concern has led three organisations with different interests in the countryside – the English Tourist Board, the Rural Development Commission and the Countryside Commission to direct interest to the issue of rural tourism.[3] The latter organisation has also issued a policy statement regarding the development of tourism, stressing the importance of conservation and highlighting development which will complement the environment rather than detracting from it.

Figure 11.1   'Green tourism'

The Tarr steps in Exmoor National Park – 'carefully erected public footpaths are essential to protect the environment from the influx of visitors'

Source: *Tourism Enterprise* (September 1990)

Thus, in terms of developing a tourism base in countryside areas it has been argued that strategies should be more environmentally aware than in the past, reflecting aspects such as new building or the re-use of existing structures, land use and heritage conservation, promotion and signposting.

At the same time, concern about tourism development has led to a series of articles and books arguing for an approach which emphasises the importance of community involvement in tourism development[4] so that an improved relationship between the visitor and host[5] can be determined.

Environmental Impact

There have also been a multitude of studies regarding environmental impact and analysis[6] which relate mainly to the impact on physical features of a landscape rather than on social and cultural aspects. Attempting to satisfy the visitor, to protect a landscape from excessive damage and to meet the needs of the host community is a difficult task, as the case study illustrates

In many places where the host community exhibits the strain of increasing visitor numbers, or where the environment is seriously under threat, policies which emphasise the reduction of demand (demarketing) tend to be adopted, but they are very few in practice. In Cumbria, the problem is being approached mainly through dispersion strategies as outlined in *A Vision for Cumbria*.[7] No one likes to mention the term 'demarketing', for it conjures an image of decline in the product life cycle. Nevertheless, marketing techniques can be used effectively to manage demand before areas become wholly saturated by the visitor: it is a term with which tourism marketeers will become more familiar by the turn of the century. The case of Derwentwater introduces practical demand management issues in such a situation.

The Case

The Peak National Park consists of 542 square miles of attractive and varied upland landscape surrounded by the major urban areas of South Yorkshire, the North West, the Potteries and the Midlands (see Figure 11.2). A staggering 20 million people are estimated to live within one hour's drive of the Peak Park. The major issue is that there are approximately 18½ million visits to the Peak Park per annum[8] of which 2 million are staying visitors and the remainder day visitors.

There are distinct visitor patterns, exhibiting seasonal and daily variations. As one would expect, approximately two-thirds of all visits are made between May and September. Sundays account for 32 per cent of summer visits and 38 per cent of all low-season visits. The flow of traffic means that Sunday afternoons are particularly busy. Visitors tend to go to the more commercial 'honeypot' areas such as Bakewell,

Castleton and Hartington although many villages and car parks throughout the park reach saturation levels by 1200 hours on a Sunday. The vast majority of visitors are sightseeing or walking (see Table 11.1 for a summary of results from previous research work).

Figure 11.2   The Peak District National Park: the regional setting

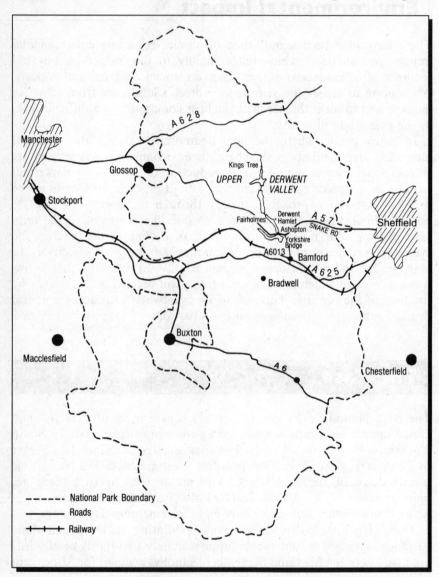

Source: Peak Park Planning Board.

Table 11.1 Comparison of 1971/2 and 1986 surveys

	1971/2	1986
1. Days of survey	24 Sundays	22 Sundays 6 Saturdays 6 weekdays
2. Hours of survey	16.00–20.00	14.00–20.00
3. Number of vehicles whose drivers or riders interviewed	2,663	11,639
4. Average car occupancy	3.3	2.77
5. Where did visitors come from (% visitors)	% Sheffield 21 Manchester 12 Derby 9 Stoke 7 Nottingham 6	% Sheffield 18.5 Gt. Manchester 15.9 Mansfield/ Nottingham 9.3 Chesterfield 5.6 Derby 3.5 Stoke 3.4
6. Proportion of staying visitors (%)	5	13
7. What time did visitors set out (%)	5 before 10.00 40 before 14.00	9 before 10.00 60 before 14.00
8. Socio-economic profile of	Amongst visitors there was a higher proportion of professional, managerial and other non-manual workers, and a lower proportion of skilled, semi-skilled and manual workers when compared to the national socio-economic profile	Amongst visitors there was a higher proportion of professional, managerial, supervisors and skilled manual workers when compared to the national socio-economic profile of car owners
9. Expenditure (1986)	£	£
Average group expenditure	6.94	9.61
Refreshments	2.70	3.64
Petrol/Fares	2.89	3.82
Admission/hire charges	0.53	0.79
Souvenirs	0.43	0.46
Other items	0.39	0.89

Source: Peak Park Planning Board.

The visitor spend is considerable. It has been estimated at £75 million[9] per annum, and this is considered to be of great importance to the local economy. However, there has been for some time a fear that visitor numbers, particularly in the most popular areas, could well lead to environmental damage and cause undue difficulties for the host population. The Derwent Dams in the Upper Derwent Valley is one such area.

In fact, the problems in the Upper Derwent began to emerge as a serious issue in the 1970s and the Peak District National Park prepared a draft Management Plan[10] for the area as a consultation document in 1979. The aims of the plan were two-fold:

(a) **Conserve the distinctive character of the area**
This would entail the formulation of land and water management policies that meet economic and functional requirements but also enhance the particular visual and wildlife character of a distinctive and popular part of the National Park

(b) **Provide appropriate opportunities for outdoor recreation**
Making the best use of the characteristics and opportunities available in the area and the management of the recreation uses to ensure that each type of activity can be accommodated in a way that minimises conflicts with other recreation uses and with land management, conservation and local interests.

The area, referred to as the Upper Derwent Valley (see Figure 11.3) comprises the higher reaches of the River Derwent and its tributaries centred on the immediate surroundings of the Ladybower, Derwent and Howden Reservoirs. It is known locally as the Derwent Dams and was made famous by the RAF 617 squadron practising their raids during the Second World War; afterwards it was used as a location for the film 'The Dambusters'.

The landscape has four main features:

(a) The reservoirs, which at the time of building earlier in the century had a tremendous impact on the environment, including the loss of a village·
(b) Enclosed farmland, occupying the lower valley levels around the reservoirs which is mainly used for sheep but some cattle are reared
(c) Woodland, dominating the valley slopes with mainly coniferous plantations but also mixed broad-leaved woodlands
(d) Moorland on the high ground characterised by rough grassland and bracken, used for grouse-shooting and grazing

---

Figure 11.3 The Upper Derwent Valley: parking and traffic management

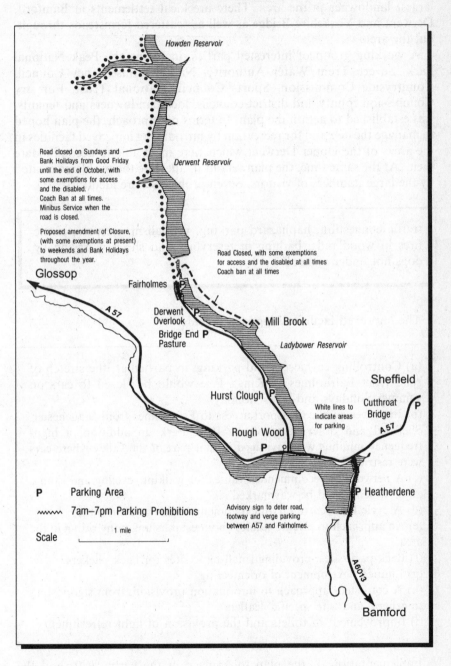

Source: Peak Park Planning Board.

The land is owned by a variety of organisations from local people to the County Council and the Severn Trent Water Authority which is the largest landowner in the area. There are local settlements at Bamford, Derwent and Yorkshire Bridge as well as scattered farmsteads throughout the area.

A working group of interested parties, including the Peak National Park, Severn Trent Water Authority, Nature Conservancy Council, Countryside Commission, Sports Council, National Trust, Forestry Commission,county and district councils, local landowners and tenants, was established to action the plan. In terms of approach, the plan hoped to manage the demand for recreation by introducing improved facilities in the areas of the Upper Derwent which were most able to accommodate them. At the same time, the plan set out to alleviate the problems created by the large numbers of visitors. Seven problems were identified:

> traffic congestion, haphazard parking, vandalism, trespass, picnic fires in woodlands, bathing in reservoirs and sheep worrying by dogs not under control[9]

The improved facilities suggested include:

> (a) Controlling car access and parking; in particular, the stretch of road from Fairholmes to Kings Tree would be closed to cars on summer Sundays and Bank holidays
> (b) Improved public transport access to Fairholmes from Manchester, Sheffield and other parts of the Peak Park; in addition, a high-frequency minibus was envisaged in that part of the valley where cars were restricted
> (c) A network of recommended routes for walking, cycling and riding, all of which would be waymarked
> (d) A cycle hire centre on an experimental basis at Fairholmes
> (e) An approach to private stables about establishing pony riding in the area
> (f) Back pack sites, providing small basic sites for back packers
> (g) Limited development of orienteering
> (h) A consistent approach to information provision, from signposting to general and 'site specific' leaflets
> (i) Improvement of toilets and the provision of light refreshments

Implementation of the plan took place in the early 1980s and the working group of organisations mentioned above won a prestigious top prize, the Royal Institution of Chartered Surveyors/*Times* Newspaper Conservation Award, in 1988 as recognition of their partnership approach in the Upper Derwent. Despite the good work, ten more years of growth in car usage has increased pressures in the valley. In October 1989 a television bulletin publicised the fact that water levels in Ladybower reservoir were so low that the remains of Derwent village were visible.

Serious traffic congestion occurred for weeks afterwards. In comparison to the usual worst Bank Holiday Monday traffic flow of 4000 vehicles and a normal summer Sunday flow of between 3000 and 3500 cars, the following counts were observed

---

Weekday – flows averaging between 3700 and 5400
Saturday – flows averaging between 5300 and 6900
Sunday – flows averaging between 6700 and 7200

Traffic jams of several miles in length occurred. This also drew attention to the tendency for 'off-peak' Sundays and weekdays to become much busier. In terms of managing demand, these figures were of great concern. Traffic counts and data regarding the minibuses were also analysed to gain further understanding of visitor arrivals (see Tables 11.2, 11.3 and 11.4).

Table 11.2   Upper Derwent minibus service statistics

	No. of passenger trips	Contacts cost (£)	Income fares (£)	Net cost cost PPB (£)
1981	1747	3125	595	2530
1982	4344	3940	760	3180
1983	4714	4475	840	3635
1984	3973	4447	810	3637
1985	2901	5213	892	4321
1986	3554	5200	990	4210
1987	3123	5330	796	4534
1988	3273	5917	736	5281
1989	4470*	5986	1350*	4636*

* October figures estimated

Source: Peak Park Planning Board.

Table 11.3 Derwent land traffic flows (car daily 2-way flow 24hr)

		1985	1986	1988	1989	1989 Av. dly
Jan	wk		495		425	
	Sat		1000		753	672
	Sun		1813		1827	
Feb	wk		220		453	
	Sat		350		768	713
	Sun		370		1959	
Mar	wk		500		773	
	Sat		900		1424	1038
	Sun		1400		1975	

(BHM fig. 4,200)

		1985	1986	1988	1989	1989 Av. dly
Apr	wk		440		510*	
	Sat		1236		1262	943
	Sun		1692		2788	
May	wk		783		(1100)	
	Sat		1003		(1500)	1429
	Sun		2250		(3000)	
June	wk	677		700	(910)	
	Sat	1092		1144	(1220)	1144
	Sun	1892		2400	(2240)	
July	wk			825	1127	
	Sat			1101	1381	
	Sun			1913	2557	
Aug	wk			1141	(980)	
	Sat			1330	(1500)	1270
	Sun			2597	(2490)	
Sept	wk	(750)			(1000)	
	Sat	(770)			(1400)	1314
	Sun	(1420)			(2800)	
Oct	wk				(2800)	
	Sat				(4300)	3414
	Sun				(5600)	

Nov	wk	360		*600*	** total est.	
	Sat	640		(1000)	786	
	Sun	1290		1500		
Dec	wk	495		*600*		
	Sat	580		(1000)	786	
	Sun	1210		1500		

Note: No figures are available for 1987.

Source: Peak Park Planning Board.

Table 11.4   Monthly average of highest daily count 1989

Site	Jan	Feb	Mar	Apr	May	June	July	Aug	Sept	Oct
SUNDAY										
Car Parks										
Fairholmes	130	41	126	132	206	160	154	184	179	185
Derwent Overlook	22	14	8	36	58	46	7	59	59	na.
Bridge End	19	7	4	18	49	29	12	28	14	51
Hurst Clough	10	9	4	10	23	15	7	16	9	na.
Roadside										
Fairholmes to										
Bridge End	na.	1	0	2	74	32	7	38	–	–
Bridge End to										
War Memorial	na.	na.	0	11	13	na.	na.	9	0	64
War Memorial										
to Hurst Clough	na.	na.	0	1	6	6	na.	4	na.	na.
SATURDAY										
Car Parks										
Fairholmes	22	23	56	91	143	103	61	129	138	na.
Derwent Overlook	na.	1	na.	3	31	5	4	7	na.	na.
Bridge End	1	2	na.	7	12	7	5	7	3	na.
Hurst Clough	na.	4	na.	5	16	14	4	9	4	

There is insufficent data for analysis of Saturday roadside parking.

Source: Peak Park Planning Board.

The Task

As a student on work placement with the Peak National Park, you have been asked to draft a short report suggesting proposals for demarketing the Upper Derwent Valley. It should include views about how the issue of traffic congestion, traffic access and parking should be addressed. You are to deliver your report personally to the working group in two weeks' time, so consideration should also be given as to how you will structure and illustrate your presentation.

References

1. R.W. Butler 'Alternative Tourism: Pious Hope or Trojan Horse?' *Journal of Travel Research* (1990).
2. B. Wheeller 'Is Responsible Tourism Appropriate?' Conference paper, Tourism Research in the 1990s (Durham University) (1990).
3. The Countryside Commission and the English Tourist Board, *Principles For Tourism In The Countryside* (1989).
4. P.E. Murphy, *Tourism: A Community Approach* (Methuen, 1985).
5. D.Gorvett, 'Tourists as Friends In The Community', Shades of Green Conference Papers (the Countryside Commission, English Tourist Board, Rural Development Commission) (1990).
6. R. Prentice, 'Environmental Analysis in Tourism', in S.F. Witt and L. Moutinho, *Tourism Marketing and Management Handbook* (Prentice-Hall, 1989).
7. Cumbria Tourist Board, *A Vision For Cumbria: Regional Tourism Strategy* (*Draft Review*) (Cumbria Tourist Board, 1990).
8. Peak Park Planning Board, *Visitor Survey 1986/87* (Peak Park Planning Board, 1988).
9. Peak Park . . . 1986/87
10. Peak Park Planning Board, *The Upper Derwent Valley: A Draft Management Plan* (Peak Park Planning Board, 19).

For a useful introduction to the issues raised in 'green tourism', see also the following three works

J. Krippendorf, *The Holiday Makers* (Heinemann, 1987).
L. Lumsdon and C. Speakman, *The Green Guide To Wales* (Green Print, 1991).

Pieda Tourism and Leisure and the Environment Task Force *Visitor Management Case Studies* (Employment Department Group and the English Tourist Board 1991.

The author gratefully acknowledges the assistance of the Peak Park Planning Board in the preparation of this case.

12 The British Tourist Authority: John Wesley's Britain

British Tourist Authority

Objectives

(a) To understand the overseas marketing task of the British Tourist Authority
(b) To practise putting together jointly financed deals
(c) To assess ways of evaluating targeted promotional campaigns

Tourism and the UK

The attraction of overseas tourists to the UK is valued in a cultural dimension, but is also vital to the economy and balance of payments. It is estimated that in 1989 17.20 million trips were made to the UK. Figure 12.1 highlights the value of international tourism to the UK during the decade 1979 to 1989. A very slight upward trend is anticipated in the 1990s but the prospect of a very unsettled Middle East following the Gulf War and world economic recession means that maintaining existing visitor numbers would be an achievement. The UK is the sixth leading visitor destination in the world in an increasingly competitive international environment. Figure 12.2 illustrates the principal tourism markets for the UK.

Overseas Visitors

Traditionally North America has been the prime source of visitors, but increasingly the European Community (EC) and other parts of the world such as Japan and Australasia are becoming important. In terms of spend, foreign tourists accounted for £2.3 billion in 1977 and nearly £7 billion by 1989, amounting to an increase of approximately 20 per cent in real terms.

Figure 12.1   International tourism volume and value

YEARLY TRENDS OF INTERNATIONAL TOURISM TO THE UK

	Area of origin			Purpose of visit				Total
	Western Europe	English Speaking	Rest of the World	Holiday	Business or Conference	Friends or Relatives	Other Persons	
TRIPS (MILLIONS)								
1979	7.87	2.84	1.77	5.53	2.40	2.25	2.31	12.49
1980	7.91	2.72	1.80	5.48	2.57	2.32	2.06	12.42
1981	7.06	2.61	1.79	5.04	2.45	2.29	1.68	11.45
1982	7.08	2.70	1.85	5.27	2.39	2.41	1.57	11.64
1983	7.16	3.39	1.91	5.82	2.56	2.56	1.53	12.46
1984	7.55	4.06	2.03	6.39	2.86	2.63	1.77	13.64
1985	7.87	4.50	2.08	6.67	3.01	2.88	1.89	14.45
1986	8.35	3.54	2.00	5.92	3.29	2.95	1.75	13.90
1987	9.32	4.18	2.07	6.83	3.56	3.18	2.00	15.57
1988	9.67	4.04	2.09	6.66	4.10	3.18	1.87	15.80
1989	10.63	4.25	2.33	7.24	4.32	3.47	2.17	17.20
NIGHTS (MILLIONS)								
1979	75	45	35	63	15	37	39	155
1980	73	41	32	58	17	38	33	146
1981	65	38	33	56	15	35	29	135
1982	65	39	32	57	15	37	27	136
1983	67	45	32	61	15	40	28	145
1984	69	52	34	67	17	41	29	154
1985	74	58	35	70	18	46	33	167
1986	75	50	33	63	19	45	31	158

table continued

NIGHTS (MILLIONS)

1987	86	56	36	73	19	50	36	178
1988	86	52	35	67	24	48	33	173
1989	91	54	41	70	24	51	40	185

SPENDING (MILLIONS)

1970	1,207	730	860	1,235	600	415	544	2,797
1980	1,248	740	973	1,258	735	457	508	2,961
1981	1,114	801	1,055	1,276	763	442	484	2,970
1982	1,161	907	1,119	1,386	794	484	518	3,188
1983	1,400	1,272	1,331	1,711	961	639	687	4,003
1984	1,563	1,642	1,409	2,052	1,091	706	759	4,614
1985	1,822	2,089	1,531	2,379	1,293	853	908	5,442
1986	2,207	1,848	1,498	2,228	1,552	844	917	5,553
1987	2,551	2,176	1,533	2,695	1,644	910	1,001	6,260
1988	2,631	2,025	1,528	2,473	1,852	922	926	6,184
1989	2,949	2,186	1,743	2,735	2,009	1,038	1,082	6,877

Source: British Tourist Authority.

Figure 12.2   Tourism from principal markets in the UK

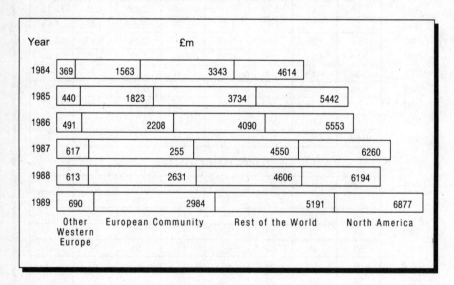

Year				£m			
1984	369	1563		3343		4614	
1985	440	1823		3734		5442	
1986	491	2208		4090		5553	
1987	617	255		4550		6260	
1988	613	2631		4606		6194	
1989	690	2984		5191		6877	

Other Western Europe   European Community   Rest of the World   North America

Source: British Tourist Authority.

The table of statistics show the value and volume of tourism by overseas residents to the United Kingdom, comparing Great Britain and Northern Ireland. Visits cover nearly all purposes, including business. Area of origin of visitors is defined by their country of residence. English speaking are those from Austrialia, Canada, New Zealand, South Africa and the USA.

The TRIPS table shows the number of visits by tourists staying one or more nights in the UK, plus one day visitors, sometimes known as excursionists.

The table heading NIGHTS shows the number of nights that overseas visitors spend in the UK, including stays with friends and relatives.

The table heading SPENDING shows total expenditure on visits, excluding fares paid to get to or leave the UK. International fare payments to UK carriers were estimated at £1,625 million in 1989.

All data are from the International Passenger Survey concluded for the Department of Employment by the Office of Population Censuses and Surveys using a very large sample of international travellers. Details and further explanation from BTA Research Services or the Department of Employment.

British Tourist Authority

The main thrust of marketing Britain abroad is in the hands of a government-supported organisation, the British Tourist Authority (BTA). The BTA was established as a national tourist organisation in 1969 with an overall responsibility to promote tourism to Britain from overseas, advise the government on tourism matters affecting Britain as a whole, and encourage improvements in tourism amenitities and facilities wherever possible.

The main objectives, as summarised in *Strategy For Growth 1989–1993*,[1] are to:

1. Maximise the benefit to the economy of tourism to Britain from abroad, while working worldwide in partnership with the private and public sector organisations involved in the industry and the English, Scottish and Wales Tourist Boards
2. Identify the requirements of visitors to Britain, whatever their origin, and to stimulate the improvement of the quality of product and the use of technology to meet them
3. Spread the economic benefits of tourism to Britain more widely and particularly to areas with tourism potential and higher than average levels of unemployment
4. Encourage tourism to Britain in off-peak periods
5. Advise Government on tourism matters affecting Britain as a whole
6. Ensure that the Authority makes the most cost-effective use of resources in pursuing its objectives

BTA Objectives

The *Strategy for Growth* sets out very clearly how these objectives are to be met:

- Collaborating with the industry and other interests to promote Great Britain as a tourist destination and encourage support for BTA's cooperative marketing activity
- Consulting with the industry and overseas sources to determine the requirements of visitors to Britain
- Researching the requirements of different overseas markets and segments to advise on product development and marketing opportunities; evaluating trends in the industry and their implications for visitor requirements
- Encouraging the provision and marketing of attractions and facilities attractive to visitors to Britain, and in particular those available in areas of higher than average unemployment and in off-peak periods
- Setting clear objectives for the Authority's own marketing activities, and measuring the results against these objectives
- Preparing and keeping up to date a strategy for the development and promotion of tourism to Great Britain from overseas
- Enhancing the status of tourism as an attractive sector of employment by stimulating education and training

---

The BTA has its headquarters at Hammersmith, London and offices throughout the world as detailed in Figure 12.3. These regional offices concentrate on establishing trade contacts in other countries, participating in travel fairs, running extensive public relations exercises and promoting current campaigns in their respective territories. They also handle thousands of enquiries from potential overseas visitors.

The BTA has in recent years been involved in numerous campaigns to encourage visitors from abroad, very often stimulating a response from certain sections of the tourism sector jointly to finance promotional campaigns such as 'Britain's Treasured Landscapes' produced with the Countryside Commission and sponsored by British Petroleum, or 'The Movie Map' sponsored by BAFTA and Shell UK.

The BTA also produces brochures and magazines of interest to overseas visitors such as a main promotional guide with 22 editions and in 17 languages. This amounts to a total print run of 2.2 million. The BTA's work in public relations is very strong; bulletins are issued regularly to

Figure 12.3 BTA world structure

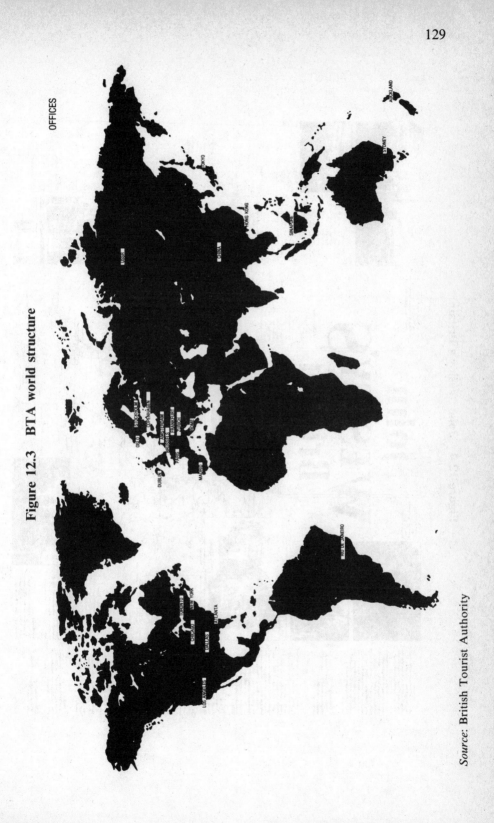

Source: British Tourist Authority

130

Figure 12.4   John Wesley's Britain

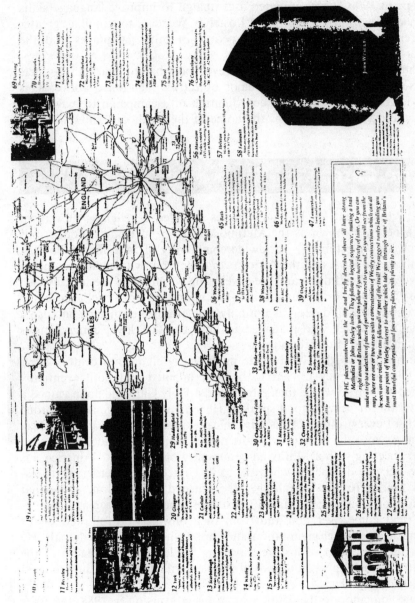

Source: British Tourist Board

overseas journalists, familiarisation trips organised, etc. The European Tourism Year campaign is a good example of such work. Not only did the BTA draw together interested parties throughout the country to become involved in preparing promotions for visitors from continental Europe in 1990, it also initiated a campaign to improve language skills for people working in tourism, ('Lost For Words'), to stimulate greater awareness of the need to train people in other languages and the understanding of other cultures.

The BTA also endeavours wherever possible to market products overseas which will meet the major objectives mentioned above. This case is about the design and coordination of a campaign to market an idea about visiting Britain as the home of the Methodist Church.

The Case

John Wesley and his brother Charles founded a religious movement which became known as the Methodist Church in Britain. Today, this church has an estimated worldwide community of 54 million followers, mainly in the USA and the African continent, but with smaller numbers elsewhere in Australasia and the developing world. John Wesley travelled some 250,000 miles throughout Britain, mainly on horseback, preaching throughout the land. He was not only a determined evangelist but also a brilliant organiser who managed to bind together loyal congregations throughout the entire country.

Born in Epworth, Humberside in the early eighteenth century John and Charles Wesley proved to be very talented and both eventually studied at Oxford where they established a Holy Club and John gained a reputation for being a good speaker. He led an austere life and recorded details of every respect of his puritanical existence in a most methodical manner, hence the derivation of the name 'Methodist'. Much influenced by his meeting with a Moravian community on his way to America, his vision became dampened when the early United States settlers took less than kindly to his preaching. He returned to London, somewhat disillusioned but on 24 May 1738 he described how a great 'Conversion' had come over him and from then onwards he followed God's calling as a preacher giving thousands hope where there was despair. He spent the remainder of his life travelling the length and breadth of the country, preaching to thousands of people until his death at the age of 87 on 2 March 1791.

To commemorate the 250th year of his conversion in 1988, the BTA investigated the possibility of putting together a Wesley Trail to market to the 54 million Methodist worshippers throughout the world. The idea of a Trail, or at least a Gazeteer, had been discussed by the marketing team at the BTA so as to stimulate 'pilgrimage' tourism. This task involved checking and resourcing an inventory of stories and information about John Wesley in Britain, a large-scale task requiring a coordinated and concerted approach. The main centres are shown in Figure 12.4 (on the previous pages).

The idea satisfied a number of criteria in terms of BTA objectives:

(1) The Methodist Church provided a clearly-defined group which could be targeted
(2) As Wesley had so many strong links with different parts of the country, such a promotion would spread the benefits to areas which would otherwise not readily attract overseas business
(3) The idea had potential for sound public relations work which would have a wider impact than the specific promotion
(4) The campaign could also be extended to include the centenary of John Wesley's death in 1991
(5) The campaign had a potential for joint sponsorship

The BTA could make the venture work only if sponsorship could be sought from interested parties. This would yield a budget commensurate with an international promotional campaign. There would have to be a budget allocated to the preparation of a trail leaflet, possibly additional publicity material and a public relations campaign. Depending on levels of support required for previous projects it was estimated that such a campaign could well cost between £35,000–£45,000, depending on the types of marketing activity employed to attract potential travellers. Sponsorship would have to meet 50 per cent of these costs for the BTA to proceed.

The Task

Following these initial discussions, you have been given the task, as a marketing assistant reporting to the marketing manager, to prepare an action programme which:

(a) Lists possible sponsors, including a rationale for your choice
(b) Suggests ways in which you intend to reach your target audience, bearing in mind budgetary constraints
(c) Recommends ways in which the effectiveness of the promotion could be monitored

References

1. British Tourist Authority, *Strategy for Growth 1989–1993* (BTA, 1988).

The following two works may also be of value.
A. Jefferson and L. Lickorish, *Marketing Tourism: A Practical Guide* (Longman, 1988) Ch. 15.
J. Heeley, 'A role of national tourist organizations in the United Kingdom', in S.F. Witt and L. Moutinho, *Tourism Marketing and Management Handbook* (Prentice-Hall, 1989).

The author gratefully acknowledges the assistance of the British Tourist Authority in the preparation of this case. Certain aspects have been amended to maintain confidentiality of data.

Index